STORIES OF BECOMING

STORIES OF BECOMING

Demystifying the Professoriate for Graduate Students in Composition and Rhetoric

**CLAIRE LUTKEWITTE,
JULIETTE C. KITCHENS,
AND MOLLY J. SCANLON**

UTAH STATE UNIVERSITY PRESS
Logan

© 2022 by University Press of Colorado

Published by Utah State University Press
An imprint of University Press of Colorado
245 Century Circle, Suite 202
Louisville, Colorado 80027

 The University Press of Colorado is a proud member of
the Association of University Presses.

The University Press of Colorado is a cooperative publishing enterprise supported, in part, by Adams State University, Colorado State University, Fort Lewis College, Metropolitan State University of Denver, Regis University, University of Alaska, University of Colorado, University of Denver, University of Northern Colorado, University of Wyoming, Utah State University, and Western Colorado University.

∞ This paper meets the requirements of the ANSI/NISO Z39.48–1992 (Permanence of Paper)

ISBN: 978-1-64642-163-3 (paperback)
ISBN: 978-1-64642-164-0 (ebook)
https://doi.org/10.7330/9781646421640

Library of Congress Cataloging-in-Publication Data

Names: Lutkewitte, Claire, author. | Kitchens, Juliette C., 1976– author. | Scanlon, Molly J., author.
Title: Stories of becoming : demystifying the professoriate for graduate students in composition and rhetoric / Claire Lutkewitte, Juliette C. Kitchens, Molly J. Scanlon.
Description: Logan : Utah State University Press, [2021] | Includes bibliographical references and index.
Identifiers: LCCN 2021035813 (print) | LCCN 2021035814 (ebook) | ISBN 9781646421633 (paperback) | ISBN 9781646421640 (ebook)
Subjects: LCSH: English teachers—Training of—Research—United States. | Graduate students—Training of—Research—United States. | Doctoral students—Training of—Research—United States. | English language—Rhetoric—Study and teaching (Higher)—United States. | English teachers—United States—Anecdotes. | Graduate students—United States—Anecdotes. | Doctoral students—United States—Anecdotes.
Classification: LCC PE1405.U6 L88 2021 (print) | LCC PE1405.U6 (ebook) | DDC 808/.042071173—dc23
LC record available at https://lccn.loc.gov/2021035813
LC ebook record available at https://lccn.loc.gov/2021035814

The University Press of Colorado gratefully acknowledges the support of Nova Southeastern University toward the publication of this volume.

Cover illustration © Macrovector/Shutterstock.

CONTENTS

ACKNOWLEDGMENTS

We are forever grateful to Nova Southeastern University for its continued support of faculty. We could not have completed this research without the help of our colleagues, administration, and research assistants. Throughout this four-year study, we were blessed to work with four talented MA students: Melissa McGuire, Jessica Organ, Salin Tilley, and Ginny Gilroy.

We would also like to thank the Conference on College Composition and Communication for funding our research through their research-initiative grant. They saw the value in exploring the transition from graduate school to the professoriate, and their funding was the impetus for this inquiry.

We would like to offer sincere gratitude to all our colleagues in this field who offered their insights in the form of survey responses, thoughtful interviews, and authentic job documents. Without the brave vulnerability of our participants, this book could not exist.

Last, this book is one about becoming—not about doing. We therefore thank all those special people in our lives for being present, attentive, and supportive of us as we journeyed from graduate school many years ago to our first full-time positions as faculty in composition and rhetoric.

STORIES OF BECOMING

INTRODUCTION

HERE'S A STORY ABOUT . . . *WHY WE NEED MORE ROBUST PREPARATION FOR THE PROFESSORIATE*

At the beginning of the 2017–2018 academic year, our faculty research team met as we often did in one of our offices on campus to discuss our research agenda for the weeks to come. For the past several years, we had been conducting a national grant-funded study on new faculty in the field of composition and rhetoric and wanted to continue with our plans for analyzing and sharing our findings. By that point, we had gathered data from new faculty across the country by surveying, interviewing, and collecting professional documents from them.

However, this particular meeting began with frustration. We had just received word from our dean that there would be cuts to our college's budget and our funding for professional development would be lowered for the upcoming year. Faculty in our college, including us, used professional-development funds to, among other things, travel to conferences to present research, collaborate on projects with peers, and speak with editors and publishers. That day, we had planned to advance our research—we had a lot to get done after all. But this news took precedence, and Juliette began with her correspondence with our dean over the cuts. She talked about the email she sent the dean that explained how the cuts to funding would make it difficult to cover the costs to attend and present at two conferences in the upcoming year, both of which involved copresenting with students. One presentation was on a service-related project with a colleague and several students; one was this grant-funded project. The dean's response was to make grant-funded projects a priority.

We were disheartened by this news of budget cuts, as it would make our own faculty responsibilities for research harder. We

https://doi.org/10.7330/9781646421640.c000

went on to talk about a disconnect between our faculty and our administration, how administration didn't understand there were not as many grants to cover the costs of conference travel available to those of us in the humanities as perhaps there were in other fields, how it was time-consuming to apply for grants in the first place, and given our course loads, not always possible. We were lucky to receive a CCCC grant to get our project funded, but even that grant wouldn't provide funding for conference travel. In total, we applied for five grants and got three for our research project, only one of which offered partial funding for conference travel.

The news of budget cuts came at a time during our research project when we were learning more about the responsibilities of the new faculty in our study, especially those in our interviews, and how those responsibilities were tied to research. We were left wondering, If new faculty members were required to participate in research, how were they supported? What resources were available to them? And it was not just about money, we realized. Certainly, financial support helped. It also helped to be given the time to do research, write, and present it. While it had been years since we researchers were in doctoral programs, we could recall that in our programs, we neither discussed ways to address something as crucial as budget cuts with college- or university-level administration nor learned that securing external funding for conference travel is a crucial but difficult endeavor. Yet these were skills we needed to advocate effectively for ourselves, as faculty members, at the moment.

The time for our research meeting was limited, so we had to set aside thoughts of the budget cuts to move on with our meeting's agenda, though those worries remained in the back of our minds.

HERE'S OUR ADVICE ABOUT . . . WHY DOCTORAL PROGRAMS MATTER TO THE PREPARATION OF NEW FACULTY

The above story is one that many faculty in the field of composition and rhetoric are familiar with, as they too have been asked to do more with less. But doing so is not something we have necessarily been trained to do through formal education. Some doctoral programs support graduate students through generous funding for professional development, but hardly are doctoral students trained to negotiate with a dean about such funding or about budgetary concerns, a lack of resources, how to find other sources of funding, and so forth. Likewise, there are a number of other situations graduate students may not be ready to handle once they become new faculty. When our study's participants described to us such situations, we knew, as researchers and as graduate program faculty, that we needed to share this knowledge with others, especially graduate students pursuing careers in our field. Composition and rhetoric doctoral programs highly value developing reflective practitioners who are active, ongoing learners, innovators, and collaborators. As a field, we aim to prepare practitioners for the dynamic demands presented in not just our classrooms and our scholarship but also in the complexities of the everyday. And that is why we wrote this book.

In 2011, Rosanne Carlo and Theresa Jarnagin Enos wrote that "at the heart of the direction and future of our field is the planning and design of our graduate programs: the classes we require students to take, the possibilities and forms we offer graduate student writing, the opportunities we create for interdisciplinary work, the professional development and outreach programs we provide for them" (210). We couldn't agree more. However, as we have found in our study, most doctoral programs still focus heavily on research and teacher training and less on the other everyday realities new professors in our field participate in. In part, this emphasis reflects the long history of and value our field places on the work we do in composition and rhetoric as practitioners—the classroom, the scholarship, the service, the leadership. While the emphasis on pedagogy in composition and rhetoric is uniquely commendable, if not exceptional, in comparison to other fields, this doesn't negate the opportunity for doctoral programs to improve, especially since doctoral programs serve as the last place new faculty receive extensive formalized professionalization.

But we also know doctoral programs can be slow to change. Therefore, we address this book most explicitly to graduate students. While we hope you aren't our only readers, we think we have the most to offer you in terms of strategies that will help you prepare for the professoriate, strategies that might not currently be afforded by your doctoral program. This text addresses six strategies:

- **Strategy 1**: Know (Y)Our Stories
- **Strategy 2**: Understand the Job Market
- **Strategy 3**: Define Your Tetrad: TRSA
- **Strategy 4**: Prepare for More Than TRSA
- **Strategy 5**: Recognize Your Time Is Valuable and Manage It Well
- **Strategy 6**: Collaborate

Through these strategies, we encourage you to collaborate with your program faculty and administrators to identify areas for improving your program for yourself, as well as future students, that go beyond training for only teaching and researching. In our research, we were reminded time and again of Virginia Crisco et al.'s work many years ago on graduate education. In their work, they argue that when we talk about graduate education, we must be careful not to see it as "the reduction of education to job training" (360). Rather, they argue that it should go beyond "training in job skills" (360) and that it should "focus as much on how students can change the profession as on how it can change them" (361) via giving students "practice in, not preparation for, the profession" (363). In other words, here is an opportunity to make a difference in the profession, while you are a graduate student, that can lead to being successful now and in your career as a professor later on. We hope you see this book as a method for viewing graduate education not as a "fixed end of professionalization" (361) but as a way of becoming a member of a profession that is, at the same time, evolving, too. Keep in mind, now and throughout the book, that when we speak of "preparation," we mean to evoke Crisco et al.'s definition extending beyond just job training to include the everyday experiences of graduate students and new faculty.

HERE'S WHAT OUR RESEARCH SAYS ABOUT . . .
CHOOSING THE PROFESSORIATE AS A CAREER PATH

Our grant-funded study spanned four years. During that time, we collected data (1) via a nationwide survey in which nearly two hundred new assistant professors in the field of composition and rhetoric participated, (2) through follow-up interviews with a sample of ten of those survey participants, and (3) by collecting professional documents (CVs, cover letters, etc.) from those interview participants. Following the collection of data, we went to work coding and analyzing using qualitative-data-analysis software that allowed us to identify themes that offered us insight into what has been working in graduate programs to prepare faculty for the professoriate and what has not. Particularly, we looked closely at what new faculty wished they had learned in their doctoral programs prior to becoming new faculty members. As new faculty learning to navigate the ins and outs of their positions, the participants were able to speak about what would have been most helpful to them prior to taking on such positions. This information was most telling because it pointed to how their doctoral programs did and did not prepare them for life as a professor.

The goal of this book, then, is to share our study's findings in order to help you better prepare for life as a professor in a multitude of ways. For the most part, our study's new-faculty participants were satisfied with their career choices, which is encouraging, as it reflects a number of things our field should be proud of. For example, when asked whether their choices would be different if they were to begin their career again, nearly 60% of participants said they would *definitely yes* or *probably yes* "choose the same doctoral program," and 67.3% said they would *definitely yes* or *probably yes* "choose the same professional path." Based on these responses, we say we are doing a good job making sure students like you in our field are happy with their choices in life regarding their careers.

Table 0.1. Survey Results: Program and Professional Choices

	Choose the same doctoral program	Choose the same professional path
Definitely yes	50	52
Probably yes	67	80
Not sure	31	32
Probably no	23	12
Definitely no	10	5
Did not answer	15	15

However, there is always room for improvement. As we discuss in this book, our field and our programs have opportunities to make real changes that can benefit everyone, not just our graduate students, though our focus in this book is certainly on you. When we better prepare new faculty, we help all faculty, and that benefits our field, our institutions, and—most important—the students we teach. Now as a professor (Claire) and two associate professors ourselves, we have benefited in a lot of ways from this research, especially in becoming more aware of the needs of our junior colleagues. Folks like us don't go into academic work because good is good enough.

In the pages to come, we discuss our findings on new faculty in composition and rhetoric, providing a picture of what successes they have had and what challenges they have faced. Our hope is that you will be able to recognize ways you can help yourself prepare for similar situations. We also hope you will be instrumental in improving doctoral programs nationwide as well as in bringing awareness to how our field educates graduate students to begin with. As was clear from our study, graduate programs are strong in some ways but have not adequately prepared students in other ways, such as for situations similar to the one described at the beginning of this introduction, the one involving budget cuts. As a soon-to-be-full-time faculty member, you should recognize that your days as a student are not finished once you graduate with your doctoral degree. Perhaps this is one of the misconceptions new faculty have. They may believe they have left formal learning behind, but on-the-job lessons can and should happen. However, unlike the more easily identifiable professionalization experienced in graduate school, new faculty are faced with the challenges of both recognizing the opportunities and creating them where they are not yet apparent. This learning should not just be the responsibility of new faculty and their hiring institutions; it should also be that of our field. Our wish for this book is that it will attest to the need for multiple avenues of support for graduate students as they transition out of their doctoral programs and into their careers as members of the field of composition and rhetoric. You will certainly play a vital role in this process, as you are currently experiencing graduate study firsthand and can share your experiences with your institution and the field now.

Finally, and more to the point, what you will find here is not only the story of our research on new faculty but how such research has helped us identify six specific strategies we believe are crucial to effectively preparing you for the professoriate. We realize there are quite a few strategies graduate students who are soon-to-be new faculty can utilize in order to be successful (more than could possibly fit in just one book). However, based on our research, it is these specific six strategies, above all, that we believe will serve you in the most productive ways as you move on to careers as professors in composition and rhetoric.

The six strategies we developed for this book came from the themes and subthemes we discovered in our data, particularly those that involved coding. Indeed, coding was an important part of our research process. We believe Rebecca Moore Howard explains the coding process best:

> Coding pushes the researcher away from confirmation bias, beyond grasping at bright shiny objects in an impressionistic reading of text. Coding compels the researcher to be systematic in handling data; it facilitates unexpected insights and impedes the researcher's impulse to notice only the passages that support his or her preliminary hypotheses. Once the coding is finished, the interpretation begins, with the researcher working with very systematically categorized and analyzed text. (79)

We were systematic in our categorizing and analyzing of the texts that contained our data and we did this through NVivo, a software program designed specifically to analyze data. What came from this coding, then, were the perspectives about our data that helped us thematically organize this text in a way that best tells our and our participants' stories, stories that illuminate ways to better prepare graduate students like you. We recognize and value the story you are bringing to this text as well and hope we can combine efforts to make our field even stronger.

HERE'S WHAT THE SCHOLARSHIP SAYS ABOUT . . . *SIMILAR STUDIES*

When we began this study years ago, our goal was to capture what life was like in our field for new faculty and, specifically, how graduate students navigate their transition to such positions as they negotiate their identity time and time again. Dozens of studies of various kinds (from case studies to surveys) about graduate programs and new faculty make calls for improvement—calls that, for the most part, continue to go unanswered. As we will discuss later, for instance, Scott L. Miller et al.'s 1997 survey on graduate students in composition and rhetoric called for graduate programs to show graduate students career options other than researching at R1 institutions. Graduate students in Miller et al.'s study also had little confidence in their future realties as professionals in the field. Such a call for more awareness of all career possibilities beyond a career at an R1 institution has been echoed time and again. David Laurence, writing in the *ADE Bulletin* in 2002, wrote that "the curriculum of doctoral education needs to educate future faculty members more directly for departments where teaching, not publication, stands at the center of what faculty members do and for faculty work as it exists in baccalaureate and two-year colleges" (14). Later, in 2014, the Committee on the Status of Graduate Students reported that graduate students had "little support in finding and considering nonacademic jobs" and that finding a job in academia can be "mystifying," especially when "many graduate students have little mentorship at their institutions for navigating the market" (1).

More recent scholarship has pointed to other shortcomings in graduate education. For instance, in their analysis of narratives from junior faculty at five different institutions who were tasked with developing an undergraduate writing major, Greg Giberson et al. warned back in 2009 that "the disparity between graduate student preparation and academic workplace realities may only become greater and more complex in the decades to come." They found that the junior faculty in their study were not entirely ready for the "challenging professional circumstances that undergraduate degree programs represent" and that, while these junior faculty were ultimately successful, there were still questions as to whether or not they could have been even more successful had "they received more direct theoretical and practical graduate instruction in undergraduate degree program development and administration." They conclude in their study that "future faculty who will develop and teach in undergraduate degrees in writing need a working knowledge of the machinery of academic production; of the specific institutional, political, and historical contexts where they will labor; of the bureaucratic, imaginative, and rhetorical work of program development; and of the possible consequences—positive and negative—of this work."

Since 2009, scholars have not just studied and made arguments about how graduate study in our field in general can improve. They have also advocated for specific areas of graduate study to improve, from focusing more "on the intellectual, on the nature of writing, on the deeply rhetorical roots of politics and ideology" (Skeffington 69), to providing "a more robust system of education and/or training for graduate students . . . interested in writing program administration" (Elder et al. 14), to rethinking doctoral program language requirements in order to steer away from "monolingualist disciplinary assumptions" (Kilfoil 441), and to arguing that "we need to listen to [graduate students'] insights, to look to their scholarship as identifying future trends" (Carlo and Enos 221). The range of studies about graduate education in our field reflects the diversity of our field and its continuous evolution.

In our study, more than twenty years after Miller et al.'s, we found that new faculty are still wishing their graduate programs had shown them career options other than researching at R1 institutions, as well as the actual realities of being a professor. What we are suggesting here is the need to do something with these studies and our own that involves more than just reading them. In what ways, we wonder, could these have a bigger impact not just on graduate students, not just on new faculty, but on all faculty and those who do and do not support faculty effectively? Our hope is that our book will encourage real change in the ways we prepare graduate students and that you will lead the way.

HERE'S HOW WE . . . *ORGANIZED AND STRUCTURED THIS BOOK*

We have devoted each chapter to one of the six strategies, providing you with a central framework to explore our research. The framework outlines each chapter in the following ways: first, each chapter begins with a story related to the strategy ("Here's a Story about . . ."), followed by advice for readers that explains why they might want to use such a strategy ("Here's Our Advice about . . ."). This strategy is the focus of the chapter, and what follows in the remainder of the chapter supports this strategy. We show how our findings from the three phases of our study led us to develop such a strategy ("Here's What Our Research Says about . . ."). We not only share statistics from our survey but also provide examples from our interviews and collected documents.

Then we discuss our field's scholarship, or lack thereof, on the subject at hand ("Here's What Scholarship Says about . . ."). After years of researching and reading studies on both graduate students and new faculty, we have included in this book scholarship you might not be familiar with from your PhD program's courses. We hope that by doing so we provide you with a wider

lens through which to view our field's stories, as well as complicate what you currently do know of them, in order to challenge
commonplaces that risk valuing certain voices, ideologies, identities, and histories over others.

After this, with the exception of this chapter, we make suggestions for how you might learn more about such a strategy
and how we might improve current programs ("Here's How
We . . ."). The two concluding sections in each chapter involve
reader participation more directly, providing you with a means
for reflection and experiential learning opportunities that have
you investigating authentic situations in the field. The first
involves answering questions and thinking about specific ways
such a strategy might be of value to you ("Here Are Questions
to Consider . . ."). And the second invites you to act, to participate, and to experience ("Here Are Moves You Can Make
to . . .") in order to better understand the strategy. We see these
last sections of each chapter serving three specific functions:
(1) demystify the professoriate, (2) compare what current new
faculty have to say of their job expectations with the realities you
might face when on the job, and (3) make visible the invisible,
behind-the-scenes work new faculty do. Our hope is that by the
end of each chapter, you will be better able to answer the questions, What will your reality be as new faculty and What is within
your power to shape it?

For a visual picture of the framework, as well as an outline
of the chapters, we provide a chart (see appendix). In addition to this visual, we have included below a brief description
of each of the six strategies to help readers prepare for the
pages to come.

Strategy 1: Know (Y)Our Stories

In other words, learn the stories important to you as an individual and to members of the field. In chapter 1, we explore
the significance of narrative and how we construct professional
identities as faculty—a process that sheds light on the experience of transitioning out of graduate school and into the

professoriate. You may be so intent on looking outward, working to establish yourself as an insider in the field and learning
its stories, that you may neglect to look inward, reflecting to
develop yourself as an individual first and foremost and understanding your own stories. If—and that's a big *if*—this study
could be generalized in one tidy soundbite, it would be values
matter—disciplinary, institutional, academic—but none matter
more than your own stories. As important as it is to experiment
with pedagogical and critical theories of teaching, research, and
academic labor while in graduate school, it is even more important that you experiment with possible selves as you construct
an identity in your profession. Learn the stories of higher education and of our field, but continue to write your own stories,
including chapters that haven't happened yet.

Strategy 2: Understand the Job Market

Understanding the field and its processes is especially important for graduate students, but perhaps no process is more
important than the job-market process. Chapter 2 uses the rite
of passage known as the *job market* to explore aspects of employment in the field that remained confusing to our participants,
even after being hired. The goal of this chapter is to make you
aware of the challenges you may face before, during, and after
you go through this process but also to suggest ways we as a field
could make this process better. Your role is to help document
this process and identify further ways to make it better.

Strategy 3: Define Your Tetrad: TRSA

In the third chapter, you will see how your future career may
revolve around how well you are able to negotiate your own
values for teaching, research, service, and administration
(TRSA)—what we refer to as the *tetrad*—with those of the institution where you work. Many of our interview participants
described having teaching loads, requirements for participating in scholarship, responsibilities for serving their departments

and universities, and even administrative roles similar to each other. However, the ways their institutions defined and evaluated this teaching, research, service, and administration varied from one institution to the next and from one person to the next. That's because much of how we define what we do has to do with what we value as individuals but also how that gets negotiated with what our institutions value. Having the wherewithal to see how this negotiation plays out on a personal and institutional level can help new faculty balance their workload and is key to being successful.

Strategy 4: Prepare for More Than TRSA

The participants in our study were particularly eager to share their thoughts about all the things that do not neatly fit into one category of TRSA. TRSA plays a dominant role in every new faculty member's life, but chapter 4 focuses on not-so-easily recognized but still important everyday activities/responsibilities new faculty participate in. These could include such things as writing a plan for a program initiative, putting together a budget for a writing program, creating marketing materials for an on-campus event, and so forth—things that matter and take up time yet are not necessarily things we clearly mark as TRSA.

Strategy 5: Recognize That Your Time Is Valuable and Manage It Well

Chapter 5 implores you to learn how to protect your time as a new faculty member and see that your priorities match your values. This chapter will help you begin practicing a work/life balance during graduate study. Our participants wished they had learned to say no—to requests for service, committee work, and so forth—and why to say no in order to protect their time. But learning to say no is easier said than done as new faculty learn what life is like when researching on their own, managing committee work, and teaching more classes than when they were in graduate school.

Strategy 6: Collaborate

Discourse communities and communities of practice have been consistent threads in our field's intellectual conversation, and the more recent public turn in composition and rhetoric suggests we will continue to critically examine our relationships with others. We are a field that values collegiality and encourages generosity and opportunities for collaboration in many forms. For our study, we were particularly interested in knowing whether new faculty participated in collaboration with colleagues, students, and community members. As we discuss in chapter 6, graduate students who participated in collaboration during their PhD program are more likely to go on to collaborate once they are in the professoriate, especially if they have collaborated in conference presentations, research with faculty, and writing grants.

Moving Forward: Faculty and Graduate Program Support

We've called the last chapter of the book not the final chapter but the moving-forward chapter, as it is a call to action, one that looks ahead to our future. In particular, we lay out three strategies for how our field, institutions, and graduate students especially can help make the transition from graduate school to the professoriate more effective for you and future graduate students in composition and rhetoric. Specifically, we see experiential learning playing a big role in this future.

HERE ARE QUESTIONS TO CONSIDER . . .
WHEN READING THIS BOOK

This book is our team's attempt to address some of the gaps in new-faculty preparation we have found in doctoral programs and move our field to action. You will not only learn about the findings of our study but also be given opportunities to apply what you learn in your own contexts, whether that be in graduate study, through mentoring, or through experiences at our field's conferences. In order to keep this goal of better preparing you as the primary focus while sharing our research findings, we have included a number of ways that provide prompts for discussion, inquiry, and action. To begin with, we suggest you develop your own list of questions about the professoriate and work with those stakeholders around you to find answers to them. We also want to offer a list of questions we feel all graduate students should consider as they think about their current situation and their future:

- What do you hope to learn as a graduate student that will help prepare you for the professoriate?
- Who or what can help you learn these things?
- What worries do you have?
- What challenges will you face?
- What are you most confident about?
- What are your strengths as a teacher? As a researcher? As a collaborator? As an administrator?
- How can you improve as a teacher? As a researcher? As a collaborator? As an administrator?
- In what ways now can you help your fellow classmates, your program, and your institution make changes to your current situation with the goal of best preparing you for a future in this field?
- What roles do graduate students play in shaping graduate programs? The field?
- What do you specifically have to offer that can create a more just, equitable, diverse, and inclusive discipline and profession?

HERE ARE MOVES YOU CAN MAKE TO . . .
KEEP AN OPEN, POSITIVE MIND

Carlo and Enos argue that "graduate core curricula give a clear indication of the trends in our field and shape our disciplinary identity as curricula reveal the knowledge(s) we value" (210), as well as contend that "social trends, disciplinary trends, and, of course, institutional resources are lines of inquiry to consider when planning a new program or revising a program" (214). As you read this book, we encourage you to think about the development of your own graduate program—its curriculum, its training, its opportunities—as it is situated in a particular institution amongst particular faculty while at the same time connected to a larger discipline comprised of colleagues who bring a diverse expertise. With the goal of helping improve your own program for yourself and future students, we hope you will consider the various aspects of graduate study that welcome us to experience the many facets of the profession and work with your faculty and administrators (as well as others in our field) to make strides in changing your current situation for the better.

In our findings, for instance, participants had a lot of experience in the areas of teaching and researching prior to taking on faculty positions but not a lot of experience in the areas of service and administration. As you begin this book, we urge you to participate in all the nitty-gritty aspects of faculty employment that go beyond teaching and researching (areas that may be a large focus of your graduate program's curriculum) and encourage your fellow graduate students to do the same. Seek the thoughts of others at your institution and elsewhere and engage in discussions about aspects of faculty employment in higher education that involve all aspects of the job.

As mentioned above, create a list of questions about your current and future plans for the professoriate as you read this book. Then, come up with a plan to learn the answers to them, whether that means finding and meeting with a mentor on a regular basis, job shadowing at other institutions in your area, or networking with new faculty at regional and national conferences. As you do, be sure you are willing to consider all possibilities for your career path and to speak with everyone about their experiences in the field whether they be tenure-track professors or adjunct faculty. Learning from others' stories is one of the most beneficial moves you can make to prepare for the professoriate and resist disciplinary commonplaces.

Strategy 1
KNOW (Y)OUR STORIES

HERE'S A STORY ABOUT . . . *HOW OUR RESEARCH REVEALED MANY STORIES*

At the end of our three-year data-collection process, our team met more often in our department's conference room than in our offices; the conference room was a wonderful space for three faculty to collaborate—several chairs circle a long table in the center of the room, a large white board consumes one wall, a screen takes up another. On one particular day, we closed the door, found seats at the table, and got started by pulling up charts from the data we had collected. We shuffled laptops, books, and handwritten notes that traced our path over the course of those three years. After we settled into our working positions, we found ourselves staring at one another as if to say, "What now?" This was our first official drafting meeting, and we weren't sure what our readers would want to know; we simply knew we needed more information in our composition and rhetoric field about what it means to transition from graduate student to professor—institutional challenges, shared concerns, small but glorious victories, contradictions, and validations included. We needed to find a path through the data; we needed to illuminate stories from our composition and rhetoric field.

We took turns talking through some of the themes and sub-themes we each had found as we analyzed the survey data and the possible connections that existed within the interview transcripts and collected professional documents of our participants. Our conversation soon took a turn away from the data, and we talked about our day—the meeting Molly had just come from, the course Juliette was trying to develop, the upcoming sabbatical

https://doi.org/10.7330/9781646421640.c001

Claire was about to take. We'd had some version of this conversation weekly for five years, and during that time we had built a support network among ourselves as we helped each other navigate new positions and expectations at our institution. Frequently, we had talked about how our lived experience, our stories, paralleled the data we had collected and the stories they told.

In fact, one of the most important findings in our research study that grounds the stories creating this book wasn't just in the data itself but was in our experience as a collaborative team. To succeed in the professoriate, we have learned, you need the people around you. This may sound rather trite, this idea that we need others, but creating a community of peers is different as a professor than it is as a graduate student. And that difference can be paralyzing. It can be enthralling. But, more often than not, it seems to be fairly confusing and a bit isolating. This realization had cemented itself for us first as new faculty ourselves and then again later on as more experienced faculty collecting the stories of others during this research study. These stories ultimately showed us why new faculty (and even experienced faculty) need others and how this need is often difficult to address. Therefore, we decided during this first official drafting meeting that our study would not be a typical textbook research write-up. We decided we needed to tell not just one but many stories so as to shed light on the many different ways new faculty succeed or don't. As Diana George writes in *Kitchen Cooks, Plate Twirlers, and Troubadours*, to paint the picture of a professor, one must tell "one story through and around many" (xii).

George's collection promises and demonstrates the very intention we have in this book: "A good story ought to send us back to the scholarship and the institutional realities with yet another important piece to the puzzle of this work . . . that is what these stories are meant to do" (xiv). Throughout this project, we researchers shared memories with one another about our time in graduate school at the same time we were witnessing each other's experiences as developing professionals teaching both undergraduate and graduate students, researching and writing scholarship, serving our college and university, and participating in administrative work. We realized that while our stories are in some ways vastly different from each other, as well as from those of our participants, they carry a multitude of similarities. The similarities kept us grounded as we developed the initial questions that ultimately guided us in crafting the survey and interview questions early on; the differences made us ask more questions than we could ever address in a single text such as this one. As our data grew, it became clear that we were not alone in our experiences and that the members of our community—professionals throughout the field of composition and rhetoric—were just as eager to share their stories with us as we were to share with each other.

HERE'S OUR ADVICE ABOUT . . . *UNDERSTANDING HOW STORIES OPERATE IN OUR FIELD*

Stories connect us, inform us, teach us. Stories have a strong tradition in composition and rhetoric. Graduate students in this field should be especially aware that we use stories in our everyday practices and scholarship; we find them in our conference presentations, writing centers, classrooms, and hallways. And these stories go beyond our job titles to our senses of self and our place in larger, dominant discourses. Pat Bizzell suggests that "there is a compelling reason for combining the personal, the professional, and the political" because as we construct our professional identities, we pull from every facet of life experience in order to do our jobs and do them well (qtd. in George vii). Maureen Daly Goggin and Peter Goggin's edited collection approaches research experiences from the perspective of stories as well, citing a much more pragmatic truth: "Storytelling through narrative structures is how humans relate to each other, pass along wisdom, and give meaning to our lives" (7). Our field's use of storytelling can help (and sometimes hinder) graduate students as they prepare for the professoriate. For instance, storytelling helps us understand why we make the choices we make, uphold or eschew certain traditions, contest or embolden different myths—how we find our way through the first few years of transitioning from student to professor and who we are on the other side of that experience. In other words, as we reflect on our stories, we reflect on who we are and who we are becoming. But in other ways, storytelling, when left unquestioned, risks privileging discourses, processes, and ways of being. While some stories may be similar or share commonalities, they may not be true for all in our field. As readers will see in this book, the participants in our study are unique, each with their own specific stories to tell that shed light on why it is important that graduate programs recognize just how diverse faculty career paths can be in our field.

HERE'S WHAT OUR RESEARCH SAYS ABOUT . . . *STUDYING NEW FACULTY*

First and foremost, what we gathered from participants were pieces of their stories, pieces that reflect the many complexities and intricacies of what it means to be a new faculty member and how our participants were prepared (or not) to be one. In other words, we examined their identities and how they constructed them. While we are keenly aware of the complexities of identity and its construction in professional spaces, we also realize demographic markers work in tandem with individual and environmental variables and feel it's necessary to share this information to help readers extrapolate additional information and narratives and to allow readers to see themselves in the data.

Of our survey's participants, 122 identified as females, 56 identified as males, 3 preferred not to say, and 15 left the question about gender unanswered. Seventy-one percent of the males and 64% of the females in our study were between the ages of 30 and 39. Five percent of the males and 10% of the females were between the ages of 20 and 29, and 9% of the males and 17% of the females were between the ages of 40 and 49. The rest of the participants were over 50 years of age. Three participants were veterans and one was active duty.

One hundred and fifty-six participants identified their race as white/Caucasian, 10 as Asian, 4 as African American/Black, 4 as

Native American/Alaska Native, 4 as Hispanic/Latinx/Chicano, 3 as Native Hawaiian/Pacific Islander, and 1 as French Canadian; 5 preferred not to identify their race. Like the graduate students in the Committee on the Status of Graduate Students 2014 report, our study's population "over-represents the general United States population in terms of women and whiteness" (6). Very similar to participants in the committee's study, our participants were majority women (62.2%) and white (83.4%).

There were 145 of these participants who indicated they were in tenure-track positions, and 31 indicated they were not on the tenure track but that their institutions had tenure. The remaining participants were in various other positions, such as on renewable contract. The majority of the participants on renewable contracts were at institutions that do not offer tenure, and the remaining participants indicated they did not have the job security offered by either of the institutional contracts (renewable contracts or tenure).

The survey participants taught at small and large public and private colleges and universities across the United States, including two- and four-year institutions. These new faculty mainly taught undergraduate courses and general education courses, as well as courses required for a major. They were less likely to teach honors or service-learning courses. More than half the participants indicated that since starting their position, they had published an article in an academic or professional journal. Nearly half of the participants indicated that since starting their position, they had published a chapter in an edited book. More than half the participants indicated that since starting their position, they had participated in academic research that spans multiple disciplines.

At the conclusion of our survey (phase 1), we had a total of 94 eligible interview participants—those who indicated on the survey that they were willing to be contacted for a follow-up interview. Since we planned to interview a total of 10 participants, we divided this eligible population into five random groups of approximately 19 respondents and used a random number generator to select 4 participants per group, hoping that among these 4, we would be able to coordinate interviews from at least 2 participants. In other words, we would interview 2 participants from each of the five groups. Just in case, we randomly selected 4 potential interviewees instead of 2 from each group in the event the first 2 we contacted within a group no longer wished to be interviewed.

We chose to conduct interviews in our mixed-methods study for a number of reasons. Interviews provided narrative accounts of faculty's experiences as professionals, thus contextualizing analysis of the collected data on the survey and providing a source for collecting professional documents (phase 3). The interviews also provided a different perspective on faculty labor that could push against or fall in line with the narratives that dominate via disciplinary lore. In the context of this study, the primary purpose of the narratives was to help us gauge the extent to which lore, historical or contemporary, was still true for the members of our field. We also chose interviews for this research project based on the research questions we were seeking to answer but also because of the reflective nature of interviews. In his book *The Research Interview*, Steve Mann writes that interviewing is a reflective practice and that "any professional activity can be better understood through attempts to reflect on practice and this is no different in the case of qualitative interviewing" (2). We felt the reflective practice of interviewing would allow the participants an opportunity to reflect and expand on their thoughts, which it did.

The following chart describes the interview participants in terms of their workload expectations. Please note we have used pseudonyms to protect their identities.

After the interviews, we went on to phase 3 of our study, which involved collecting professional documents from our interview participants. In total, we collected thirty-one documents, which included CVs, cover letters, teaching philosophies, self-evaluations, reflections, and research agendas, documents that served as a textual means with which we could analyze new-faculty identities and the ways that developing professionals represent their careers in composition and rhetoric.

Table 1.1. Interview Participants and their Workload Expectations

Interview Participant	Teaching Expectation	Administrative Expectation	Research Expectation	Service Expectation
Bailey	4/4	WPA	Yes	Committee work; dept., college, univ. service
Sam	4/4	No	Yes	Committee work; some WPA support
Casey	4/4 with 1/1 release	No	Yes	Committee work; dept., college, univ. service
Jamie	3/3	No	Yes	Dept. service
Tahir	3/3	No	Yes	Committee work; dept., college, univ. service; administrative work
Lee	2/3	No	Yes	20% of load
Dev	2/2	Writing Center	Yes	20% of work week
Alex	2/2	No	Yes	Committee work; mentoring
Kai	2/2	No	Yes	Committee work; dept., univ. service
Rey	3/3 with 1/1 release	Writing Center	Yes	50% of load

The majority of the study's participants primarily identified themselves as teachers of writing, speaking time and time again about their experiences in this particular role. We were not surprised they identified as teachers of writing, given the centrality of practice in our field. What was surprising, however, was how such an identity was complicated and/or complemented by participants' identities as researchers, colleagues, citizens, stewards, and administrators of their institutions. Moreover, we were surprised by the *ways* identities were in constant flux as participants negotiated time, resources, and expectations in their new institutional contexts.

Research methods employed by past studies on the construction of identity have included both quantitative and qualitative methodologies. For instance, in their longitudinal qualitative study on constructing professional identity, Michael G. Pratt, Kevin W. Rockmann, and Jeffrey B. Kaufmann conducted semistructured interviews, surveys, archival analysis, and observations (239). In our study, we planned to extend the work of previous scholarship to acknowledge the impact of not only teaching but also research, service, and administration in the formation of new faculty members' professional identities and the stories faculty tell. We wanted to determine particular rhetorical strategies employed by new faculty members in order to advance knowledge regarding professional-identity development in higher education, specifically in the field of composition and rhetoric. We knew a mixed-methods approach would best help us do this. We also knew collecting one type of data would allow us only narrow views of professional identity; we needed the big picture. We needed to see faculty identity within departmental, institutional, economic, political, and cultural contexts. Speaking about new literacy studies (NSL), Gloria Jacobs writes that "the researcher's gaze must continually shift from the local to the global. As such, data collection must focus on the local but do so with the knowledge that local data does not stand alone and needs to be contextualized" (334). In this way, our study continually examined individual participant narratives within the larger discourses of composition and rhetoric, as well as higher education.

In addition to our narrative inquiry into our participants' identities and stories, we saw our study as phenomenological. While research on professional-identity construction has largely relied on individuals and narrative study design (Hallier and Summers; Slay and Smith; Stein et al.), phenomenological research attempts to describe the phenomenon in ways that contribute to generalizability. It is our hope that this generalizability will be useful to you as you transition into the professoriate, but it is by no means a meter stick against which to compare yourself. While overlap was certainly observed in our data, it was clear there are as many unique paths in this career as there are professionals in composition and rhetoric. Honor your path as uniquely yours.

Moreover, as time passed, our research revealed many of the nuances in how research gets done, and we found that, while we were interested in our participants, we couldn't help but engage in ongoing reflection on our own identities, particularly in the context of this project. Because of the collaborative nature of our study—researchers working together along with a network of resources—it was hard for us to ignore the idea of research-as-action because we were accountable not only to the inquiry but also to one another as colleagues. Balancing the responsibilities we had beyond this research and supporting one another within our department informed decision-making at every turn. To that end, we did not see ourselves as separate from the research we were conducting because *how research gets done* was always at the forefront of our thoughts and actions; research, like any faculty task, must be planned in advance, revised as it unfolds, and negotiated as objectives are or are not met.

In narrative inquiry, researchers are not separate from the research but are very much an integral part of it. As a result, this book is about the process of researching, what we learned from discovering and creating these narratives, and how we can highlight the processes of researching for you, our field's graduate students in particular, who will also likely want to use narrative in our field. Woven together, the narratives of our participants and the narratives of our research speak to a much larger story, one integral to composition and rhetoric. Joanne Addison writes that "the heart of identity narratives is not a process of description or even drama per se (á la Kenneth Burke). Rather, these narratives are rooted in a recursive process of becoming, where the orientation and complication may change while the evaluation increases in complexity and the resolution may, or may not, differ through time" (376). Thus, we have viewed our research as recursive. The research has shaped us as much as we have shaped our research, and all continue to evolve.

While the narratives of our research cannot be divorced fully from the narratives of our participants, we do not wish to argue that, in weaving together our participants' stories with our own, we are telling *the* stories of the field. Quite the contrary. Much of our intention here is motivated by a need to populate composition and rhetoric with micronarratives and a resistance to disciplinary lore about the job market, hiring processes, and new-faculty transition. We realize each of our study's participants come from different cultures, departments, programs, and institutions, as well as different social, political, and economic backgrounds, all of which make their circumstances unique. Similarly, we realize our researcher stories are built on our unique experiences in the discipline and in our culture and are shaped by the social, economic, and political interactions we have at our university and beyond. We believe the following chapters highlight the ways our stories connect with and diverge from the larger narrative sustained through scholarship, practices, and conversations within our field.

HERE'S WHAT SCHOLARSHIP SAYS ABOUT . . . *NARRATIVES AND STORYTELLING*

Narratives have a long interdisciplinary history and are not new to composition and rhetoric (for a brief interdisciplinary history, see Addison). However, we are conscious of what has been said about them in our field. Debra Journet, for example, has argued that we must be cautious with narratives because "the stories we tell about ourselves . . . are at least partly stories we have been acculturated to tell" (16). We echo Journet's assertion that, as a field, we have learned to build narratives in certain ways that can sometimes prohibit us from constructing narratives that are truly authentic representations of the stories we wish to share. We are also cognizant of our inner rhetorics, those "stories we tell ourselves about ourselves, our tacit beliefs about how the world works or doesn't" (Mathieu 180). As a result, we see the narratives written in this book as unfinished, or rather *without end*, because of these existing, persistent limitations.

These stories are not complete—they do not capture every minute, every utterance, every piece of our research story or the stories of our participants. They did not happen once upon a time. They are still happening and will continue to happen. Recalling Journet, we are reminded that "researchers select (out of everything they know to have happened) those events they deem most significant and arrange them in terms of their temporal and causal relations. The resulting narratives interpret the past from the perspective of the researchers' present (their methodological, theoretical, and rhetorical commitments)" (17). Thus, this book is our attempt at using specific narratives, ours and our participants', to tell stories still being lived.

We did not set out to be narrative inquirers, but we became—and are continuing to become—narrative inquirers along the way. The deeper we delved into this project, the more we realized we were not just looking at data points, or numbers on a survey, or coded words devoid of humanity. What we were looking at were fragments of an individual's story. And, as we recognized the similarities across our participants' shared experiences, we acknowledged the many stories that collectively make up our discipline. Clandinin et al. contend that "people shape their daily lives by stories of who they and others are and as they interpret their past in terms of these stories. Narrative inquiry, the study of experience as story, then, is first and foremost a way of thinking about experience" (24). The ways we looked at our data, the ways we *thought* about them, was indeed a story about experiences both of the discipline and its members. We came to see ourselves participating in many of the experiences expressed by our participants, reflecting on the differences and questioning the similarities.

While we recognize there are far too many stories about graduate program development and new-faculty development to share in just one book, we would be remiss in this chapter about stories not to point out any. Therefore, we share a few specific stories that can offer different perspectives for the ways our field has shaped graduate study over the years, PhD programs in particular, and the ways we prepare new faculty. Our interview participants saw the importance of story and spoke about their experiences in the field developing their professional identities. In telling her story, for example, one interviewee, Tahir, explained, "Everybody comes to the profession with tons of experience and qualifications, and I think holding your professional identity is a matter of figuring out what am I going to prioritize out of this, how am I going to present myself, and how am I going to present the contributions I can make to the field." Another participant, Casey, revealed her professional identity through the story about her job. "I understand my professional identity," she contended, "is sort of like my outward-facing, my job. My job and what I do with the majority of my time. What it looks like on my business card. I think that's my professional identity." While rhetoric and composition's community members maintain diverse experiences and practices, what we do with our time and how we make sense of that time is integral to learning how we present ourselves within and beyond our institutions and our field of study.

In addition to the studies we have already mentioned, we would also like to point to Jillian K. Skeffington's 2010 study of doctoral programs in composition and rhetoric for its examination of the last fifty years, which takes into consideration "trends in the discipline" and the "institutional spaces we occupy" (67). She paints one history useful to those who want to get a sense of how PhD programs came to be in the field. As you will read later in this book, narrative accounts such as those by Ashton Foley-Schramm et al. and Greg Giberson et al. provide perspectives on how graduate students and new faculty learn to do administrative work.

We can also turn to scholarship directed to academia in general for its stories of what life is like for new faculty. Darla J. Twale's *A Faculty Guide to Succeeding in Academe* provides plenty of stories that involve new faculty and how they must navigate the various situations they encounter. In chapter 2, for example, Twale describes the experience of a new assistant professor asked to head up a search committee for the first time. As the scenario unfolds, readers get a glimpse at what thoughts and questions new faculty must contend with when put in positions they are not yet ready for. Ultimately, after consulting with a mentor, the new assistant professor turned down the chair position for the committee but participated instead as a committee member. In the event you are placed in a similar position, stories like this one might help you make an informed decision.

HERE'S HOW WE . . . *USE STORY TO REFLECT ON PROFESSIONAL IDENTITY*

While narrativizing identity risks creating a static image of *being*, we see this book aligning with ontological narrative; it is stories of *becoming*. Although many of us find ourselves telling a similar story or stories throughout our careers—accounts of what it means to balance research and service expectations, illustrations of navigating institutional politics, vignettes of a teaching life—these life narratives are no more fixed than their narrators. The recursive nature of both the moment and its retelling allows us to revise the story in light of reflection. Because our participants are in a transitional space, forming and shaping identity through lived experiences, in many instances, this research captures some of their earliest reflective moments as they began their positions as faculty. Some of the interview questions seemed to be new lines of inquiry for the faculty members themselves. For example, another participant, Lee, noted that the reflective questions throughout the interview felt "like a test," and while Casey struggled to define concepts such as professional identity and institutional citizen, she acknowledged them to be part of her lived experience.

Part of our research into faculty-identity construction was to identify how participants used their experiences to develop their own understanding of professional identity. At times, participants were conscious of how defining their identities could affect their work as teachers, researchers, and institutional citizens. One of the challenges we faced with our population of new faculty was that, in order to get a phenomenological sense of how identity is constructed for new faculty, we needed a sense of the sociotemporal context each faculty member came from and went to—a sense of the academic and disciplinary culture they grew up in and how that might differ from where they landed. While lore is somewhat controversial, and perhaps even problematic, we knew using lore as part of our framework would allow us to acknowledge we are capturing practitioner and community-member stories, or micronarratives, and provide the kind of data flexibility and material variation needed to illustrate identity construction. Essentially, we agreed that statistical data would not fully capture the process of identity construction and that narratives would be key to understanding how we perform identity dynamically in the kinds of situations facing faculty as they transition out of one environment and into another.

What we discovered is that there is no single new-professor narrative—our graduate-school experiences are as diverse as our job-market experiences, and our hiring institutions each hold different expectations and offer various levels of support as we learn to navigate our new roles. Over the course of a few months, our initial assumption that we needed a methodology as flexible (but sustainable and reliable) as these experiences became a somewhat pressing reality. Our data and research materials needed to be cohesive but offer different ways into the work of constructing identity and reflecting on professional expectations and goals. Recognizing that this was, in many ways, ethnographic research, we turned to a balanced mixed-methods approach so we could gather quantifiable data that would be guided contextually by concepts of narrative, phenomenology, and historiography.

Indeed, reflection played a key role in our and our participants' stories. Another participant, Jamie, noted at the end of his interview, "I dug things up as you [asked questions], things I hadn't thought about." Each participant individually and uniquely embodied signifiers of early reflection while demonstrating its impact on their understanding of how identity is shaped through not only their experiences but also their retelling(s). As a result of its recursivity, identity is fluid and reiterative; we use stories to make sense of these experiences and compose a *self* of possibility (for more on this, see Judith Butler, *The Psychic Life of Power*).

One of our goals with this project was to capture the moments we believed would become a part of that professional-life narrative and spotlight key themes and subthemes in order to gain a sense of our collective disciplinary possibility. Through our research, we hoped to not simply retell a series of thematic narratives but to construct a sense of where, as a field, we have been, where we are, and where we might go from here.

Several scholars support the exigence for revisiting our disciplinary narrative through the micronarratives of our community members in the professoriate. As Jerome Bruner deftly notes, "As everyone from Aristotle to Kenneth Burke has noted, the impetus to narrative is expectation gone awry" (28). Through our stories, we identify the chaos that may or may not have led to success, the complications that arose through our journey, the Burkean *trouble*. In the retelling, we learn. Bruner's work argues that our story isn't just within us but is also in the pieces of our community we internalize and integrate in our stories. We are not simply stories of our personal experience; we are stories of our community, our social and cultural experiences. Moreover, when our stories are brought together, they "conventionalize the inequities" and "contain the imbalances and incompatibilities" we experience as members of that community, society, and culture (93). While we do not attempt to prescribe academic culture, we believe this text offers a significant understanding of the ways burgeoning practitioners navigate those inequities and negotiate the incompatibilities. To tell or bear witness—within a discipline, or in a more personal encounter—is to coconstruct identity at individual, communal, cultural, and ideological levels. Thus, narratives, be they big or small, perform the precise function required for identity-construction inquiry.

HERE ARE QUESTIONS TO CONSIDER . . .
WHEN THINKING ABOUT STORIES

Think about your experiences thus far in the field, from going to class to going to conferences, from speaking with professors to speaking with classmates, from reading textbooks to reading Web texts. Carlo and Enos write, "The study of core curricula is also essential to understanding our disciplinary identity; it is a way of looking through the kaleidoscope to see the changing narrative dimensions of the field" (220). As you think about these experiences, think critically about your own program's core curriculum and its role in shaping the field. What role do you play in this changing narrative? While you work to find answers to these questions, we offer here some additional questions to keep in mind:

- What stories of the field have you come to know and how?
- Who wrote these stories?
- Who didn't write these stories?
- How are stories valued in the field?
- What roles do researchers play in the writing of such stories?
- What roles do graduate students play in the writing of such stories?
- How do these stories shape your doctoral program?
- How do they shape your preparation for the professoriate?
- How does your doctoral program shape the field?

HERE ARE MOVES YOU CAN MAKE TO . . .
REFLECT ON YOUR AND OTHERS' STORIES

To find stories evolving now, interview new faculty members at your institution and those institutions that differ from your own. In other words, we encourage you to locate new faculty at a wide range of institutions and find out what life is like for them. Develop a list of questions you can ask these new faculty members to learn more about what they do on a daily basis, what challenges they face, what successes they have had, what was surprising to them when they entered the professoriate, and so forth. If you are reading this book for a class, consider sharing your findings with your classmates.

Next, examine the field's stories by reading the work it produces. Books, journals, Web texts, and so forth are rich with stories from our field. In their study of a graduate seminar course, Crisco et al. describe a project involving the mapping of disciplinary conversations in the journals of a given field (364). Drawing from this study, we want to suggest you map out the stories you see in our field's publications, whether journals or books or Web texts or some other form of publication, so you may see the ways stories are written, read, and discussed and how they shape our institutions and our practices in graduate education.

After you have interviewed others and have investigated written stories, take some time to get to know your own stories better through personal reflection. For example, to help you know your story, write it. Keep a journal—written, visual, or oral—in which you reflect on your experiences in the profession and your current graduate program. Share your story with others and compare how your story is different and/or similar to theirs.

Because dissertations are often the culminating work of graduate study and are often responsible for changes in core curricula as they "anticipate the flow and direction of the field" (Carlo and Enos 210), we end this section with one last prompt. That is, we want you to examine the role your dissertation will play in our field's story. How will it change the narrative? How will it change the future of your program and the programs at other institutions? How does it shape your story?

Strategy 2
UNDERSTAND THE JOB MARKET

HERE'S A STORY ABOUT . . . *THOSE ON THE JOB MARKET*
In the middle of a meeting room, graduate students and faculty in the field are gathered at tables and are waiting for us to begin. Our research team has come to this room to cofacilitate a workshop sponsored by the 2018 CCCC's Committee on the Status of Graduate Students. Working with Beth Keller, who is doing research on how, with "the help of mentoring, people form relationships that influence their ability to learn and transfer knowledge over the duration of their career" ("About Me"), our research team is tasked with leading the first activities. After quick introductions, Molly heads to one of the tables with a stack of images in her hand. She sets the images down, spreads them out, and says, "We would like to begin by having everyone choose one image to represent their feelings about the job-market experience."

The audience members hesitate a moment before moving from their seats and examining the images. There are images of people with terrified faces, people shouting, people jumping for joy, and people smiling. After a few minutes, everyone has chosen their representative image. Most workshop participants take images that reflect feelings of fear, uncertainty, being overwhelmed, and frustration. A few take images that remind them to be hopeful.

Molly asks if anyone would like to share their reason for choosing a specific image. A couple of people in the audience share their stories while others listen and nod their heads as if to say they, too, have similar stories to tell. As the morning goes on and we move into group discussions and activities, more people

https://doi.org/10.7330/9781646421640.c002

open up and share their experiences preparing for and navigating the job market.

"I've applied to over thirty jobs," one participant says.

"Me too," another says. "And I still don't have a job. I feel so frustrated. I don't know what to do. My advisor says to hold out for a tenure-track position at an R1, but I don't know anymore."

HERE'S OUR ADVICE ABOUT . . . *THE*
JOB-MARKET EXPERIENCE

Although our study only examined one type of academic position—full-time assistant professors—the variety of institutions and their cultures in which these professors taught has made clear the diverse roles faculty assume under the ubiquitous title of *assistant professor*. Rhetoric and composition graduate programs, thus, would do well to prepare students for a variety of faculty responsibilities, not just full-time tenure-track research positions at R1 institutions. (While "R1" is no longer used by Carnegie, it is used colloquially within our field. Because our participants often used this term, we chose to use it in our book when referring to very-high-research-activity schools.) Many of our participants echoed this sentiment, wishing their graduate programs had taught them about options beyond the R1 research position, including those outside academia, especially because the job-search process was a frustrating one. Finding an R1 research position is like finding a needle in the haystack. In reality, students are seeking a variety of other positions. In fact, the Committee on the Status of Graduate Students reports that "nearly one-third expressed interest in teaching at community colleges" and "13% expressed interest in non-tenured teaching" (9). Not only that, but as research has shown, "graduate students go to graduate school for a variety of reasons, including personal reasons like love of learning and research interests, professional reasons like wanting to teach, and economic reasons like job security and advancement"; at the same time they look beyond academia for jobs (Committee on the Status of Graduate Students 9).

Thus, the job market is likely one of the most unpredictable and complicated professional experiences many of us will ever face as we transition into faculty positions, if that kind of position is what we seek. In addition to the loneliness expressed by the workshop attendees in this chapter's introduction, the uncertainty of the market reaches beyond whether or not a tenure-track line will be available. As one of our study's participants, Lee, noted, "Even in grad school, I think going on the job market, you aren't quite sure if people who are on hiring committees will be okay with your professional identity because you're questioning almost everything about it."

When on the job market, we represent ourselves in particular ways, highlighting the work we've accomplished and work we want to do, but how do we know we will get the job? And once we have it, how do we know we will be a good fit? How do we know whether we are negotiating our professional identity in ways true to the image presented on the market? How do we know the identity we put forward during this experience is what the field needs or wants? While we cannot answer these questions definitively in this book, we hope to shed light on some of the intricacies of the market and how it impacts the ways we shape our faculty identity on the other side of it.

While you should understand what you are up against when you go on the market, you should not compromise who you are, and graduate programs (and hiring institutions) should support you for who you are and the diverse qualities you bring to the table. Seek out a network of people who can help you stay true to yourself and advocate for you, as well as support you while on the job market.

HERE'S OUR RESEARCH ABOUT . . . *HOW PARTICIPANTS FELT ABOUT THE JOB MARKET*

In addition to the four overarching research questions that guided us, plenty of other questions helped shape our project. For instance, because we wanted to study the experiences of new faculty, at the onset our attention centered on answering

one important question: How do we find new faculty members
to study? We thought about different ways we could locate and
then reach this population, but one way stood out as the most
effective and efficient: using the job market. The job market
unites composition and rhetoric scholars and practitioners and
garners our field's constant attention to the point it has become
a professional rite of passage. It is a resource for both new community members and existing members, provides insight to our
field's positionality and value within the larger institutional system, and offers a snapshot of the field's identity and the identities of its practitioners.

There are several ways to go about looking for a position in
our field, and we thought that utilizing these means would be
beneficial to our research. As one example, to find our population to study, we started by looking at the online calls for full-
time assistant positions in our field, specifically those posted to
the Academic Jobs Wiki for the field from 2013 to 2015. Faculty
who were hired for these positions would most likely be new faculty members in their first three years of full-time employment,
thus applicable to our study's population needs, and they would
also be those who were closest to the job-market experience,
offering a more complete understanding of how professional
identity is both informed by and presented during this vital step
toward transitioning into the professoriate.

The job market also proved useful in the third phase of our
research project, which helped contextualize both the field's
identity and that of its community members. We used the job
market to gain a sense of the kinds of identity markers and
narratives rhetoric and composition values and to gather and
analyze materials from participants that reflect how one identifies oneself as a faculty member in our field. Among the participants' materials, for instance, were their CVs, cover letters,
and teaching philosophies because these were the materials
most often requested by hiring committees; these are cast as the
field's most valued narratives by their recurrence in job-market
calls. As such, these documents are designed to spotlight different elements of our field's community identity: how and what

we teach, the kinds of service we do, where and how we focus our research, communities and organizations we participate in, where and how we engage as leaders, and so on. Moreover, we design them to represent our individual identity as a potential faculty member in our field.

In the survey phase of our study, 75.1% of participants either *agreed somewhat* or *strongly agreed* that faculty in their doctoral programs helped students develop an effective strategy for the job search. Moreover, 90.2% of participants reported that their doctoral program *expected students to conduct an academic job search*, indicating this process remains a staple in many composition and rhetoric doctoral programs nationally. During phase 2, the interviewing stage of our study, participants talked at length about their graduate school education; these conversations uncovered a number of insights about the job market and how participants were prepared (or not prepared) to find, apply for, and obtain a job once they graduated from their doctoral program. We found that many participants did receive some form of preparation in their programs. For instance, Jamie's experience involved "professionalizing the grad student via a required seminar about the profession and professional issues." He explained that grant funding was given to graduate students so they could go to conferences and network with well-known people in the profession. Kai, on the other hand, spoke of specific types of conversations included in her graduate program for job-market preparation: "My program was really great at prepping all of the students, including me, for the demands of the job market and some of the conversations that might come up with issues associated with pay or being a woman and being a teacher and being a researcher."

While participants appreciated the kinds of experiences in graduate school that prepared them for the job market, several participants indicated their programs portrayed the job market as a difficult endeavor. Rey's responses about what she learned in graduate school represented this portrayal. She said the professors "talked about how terrible the job market was" and were "very honest about that." However, Rey was able to work on

Table 2.1. Survey Results: Job Search

With the final term of your doctoral program in mind, rate how strongly you agree or disagree with the following statements:

	Agree Strongly	Agree Somewhat	Disagree Somewhat	Disagree Strongly
I worried that I would not find a job during my search.	91	54	23	13
I developed a fall-back plan should I not find a job during my search.	59	60	32	30

search committees and said that experience "certainly taught [her] what it was like to be on the job market and the kind of performance that [she] needed to develop there." According to our participant interviews, graduate programs were teaching survival skills for a rather undesirable job market. In phase 1 of our study, we asked participants specific questions related to the job search. Notably, 78.3% of survey participants either *agreed somewhat* or *strongly agreed* that faculty helped them "develop an effective strategy for the job search." However, table 2.1 suggests that even with supportive faculty and a strategy in place, employment concerns remain prominent among doctoral students.

As indicated in this table, the majority of our study's participants worried to some degree (and rightly so) about not finding a job. Coupling this data with our research on the state of the market, it seems composition and rhetoric doctoral faculty are taking responsibility for providing graduate students with a realistic outlook on their prospects. However, we remain concerned that, even with faculty and program support, framing the job market as something to survive shares some responsibility with the institutional practices that make it daunting and worrisome.

When asked to talk specifically about what shaped their professional identity, several participants turned to the job market as a key tool in constructing their professional identity. While Annie S. Mendenhall's research on job ads focuses on compositionist specialists and the misdirected belief that the diversity in what compositionists can specialize in is ultimately detrimental to the field, her work suggests the job market does play a part in the way we shape our professional identities. We find her discussions of expertise pertinent to our participants' conceptions of professional identity, as such an identity is, in part, constructed by one's expertise. In addition, Mendenhall suggests we should look beyond the job ads and the job market to understand what we do and why we do it, contending that "we need to interrogate how our location, faculty positions, and labor structures shape our expertise—historically, theoretically, and pedagogically" (13). Tahir, for example, thought of professional identity in terms of "how you sell yourself when you're on the job market," saying that "everybody comes to the profession with tons of experience and qualifications, and I think holding your professional identity is a matter of figuring out 'What am I going to prioritize out of this?' 'How am I going to present myself?' And 'How am I going to present the contributions I can make to the field?'" Jamie had a similar response: "Thinking back to going on the job market . . . [I] think of how I had to create a certain kind of identity, particularly online."

When Bailey discussed professional identity, he talked about it in terms of "being a good rhet comp citizen in many ways," saying being on the job market means being a "professional" who can speak really clearly about how to teach survey courses in composition and rhetoric and how to be "the jack of all trades that most institutions need." A belief in the importance of a candidate's diverse capability has been a characteristic of our field for decades, as Mendenhall shows in her analysis of job ads from the 1960s to the 1980s that call upon flexible expertise.

Tahir, however, thought her professional identity didn't develop until she was actually on the job market. She said, "Once I started actually applying for positions, I started envisioning myself . . . filling a certain role and I think that was when I really started to think about my professional identity." She also noted that professional identity could change after the job market once one becomes a faculty member.

[Pedagogy research is] one thing I did a conference presentation on this year that had nothing to do with the professional identity that I had formed or had presented on the job market. But it was something that was very pressing that a colleague and I recognized was an issue in our program, and so that research was very, kind of, department-based, and we haven't published it yet for a broader [audience], but we could certainly do that. I'd love to do that. But again it took me away from being able to present research in my research area. So I'm still wondering is that the right move?

As Bailey and Tahir suggest, our field currently illustrates a narrative that requires both specializing and generalizing. The contradiction creates a complicated space for professional identity—to learn to do one well, must we sacrifice the other? If we engage in research outside our specialty, will that damage the possibility of being hired? Of later getting promoted?

Being on the job market was a personal learning experience in crafting a professional identity for many of our participants, some of whom found the experience quite liberating. Alex, for instance, said, "I learned that, while on the job market, people just don't want to know your qualifications; they want to know if you're the kind of person they want to work with for the next few years. And so that was tremendous because then I felt more comfortable about being myself while on interviews and on campus visits, and I think it paid off. I think it led to more success."

During our research over the past several years, we had countless conversations about what it means not only to become faculty but also, more specifically, what it means to obtain a position in our field. Our interview participants often talked at length about the transition they made from graduate school to full-time employment, a transition that goes directly through the job market. Such a journey has many different effects on professional identity, which illuminates how those in our field use the job market to obtain a job, what the job market says about what is valued in our field, and how it impacts your graduate school education.

HERE'S WHAT SCHOLARSHIP SAYS ABOUT . . . *JOBS*

Examining the Modern Language Association's (MLA) *Job Information List* (*JIL*), Mendenhall offers one lens for looking at the trends in faculty positions in our field. In her research, she examines early job advertisements for composition "specialists." Her goal is to confront arguments that our field has too many areas of expertise, which ends up making our field different from other fields that have clearly defined, specific specialty areas. In doing such research, she too suggests we might consider preparing graduate students for jobs outside academia. Mendenhall writes that

> composition's ability to adopt multiple areas of "expertise" has facilitated the growth of professional writing, technical writing, and digital media studies—specializations that have diversified the field in profitable ways, but that challenge the boundaries between academic expertise and occupation. Composition's extension into these fields might offer a useful way to prepare graduate students for professions outside of academia, and ensure that our graduate education provides students with flexibility over which they can exert some control. (27)

Agency matters and, regardless of what side of the market you are on—whether it's beginning to prepare a market dossier or preparing for the first days of the dream job—finding ways to embody the professional identity you have been cultivating can be difficult and likely will require some creative approaches to both the job market and your new-faculty experiences.

A look at recent studies on faculty growth rates, as well as degrees granted by institutions, can help us better understand the state of academia. Several studies, for instance, seem to suggest that part-time positions are more common today than they were just a decade ago. According to *The Condition of Education 2017* report, written by the US Department of Education, Institute of Education Sciences, and the National Center for Education Statistics, from fall 1995 to fall 2015, the total number of faculty at degree-granting postsecondary institutions increased by 66% (from 932,000 to 1.6 million). The percentage of all faculty who were female increased from

40% in 1995 to 49% in 2015. The number of full-time faculty increased by 47% (from 551,000 to 807,000) over this period, compared with a 95% increase in the number of part-time faculty (from 381,000 to 744,000). As a result of the increase in the number of part-time faculty, the percentage of all faculty who were part time increased from 41% to 48% over this period. However, between 2011 and 2015, the number of full-time faculty increased by only 6% (from 762,000 to 807,000), while the number of part-time faculty decreased by 2% (from 762,000 to 744,000) (254). While these numbers may at first seem to paint a different picture from the one in which Rey's professors prepared their students for a "terrible" market, keep in mind that the Modern Language Association's 2014 "MLA Survey of Departmental Staffing" reports 17.2% of department faculty are in full-time tenure-track positions, while 49.9% are part time and nontenure track; education-based employment is possible, but the traditional notions of what professorial positions look like has certainly shifted.

The Delphi Project (University), a project of the Pullias Center for Higher Education at the University of Southern California in partnership with the Association of American College and Universities, confirms that

> Whereas full-time tenured and tenure-track faculty were once the norm, more than two-thirds of the professoriate in non-profit postsecondary education is now comprised of non-tenure-track faculty, many who encounter working conditions that constrain their capacity to provide the highest quality instruction and educational experience for their students. New hires across all institutional types are now largely contingent.

To put this in perspective, of the 196 survey participants in our study who reported their employment-line category, approximately 74% held tenure-track (TT) positions and 16.3% held nontenure-track (NTT) positions at institutions with a tenure system in place. This suggests that although the university system may be moving away from tenure-based structures, many graduates in composition and rhetoric continue to find tenure-track jobs.

In order to gain insight into the likelihood of institutions moving forward with new-faculty models that differ from the current models utilizing tenure-track faculty and adjuncts, Adrianna Kezar, Daniel Maxey, and Elizabeth Holcombe surveyed faculty, campus administrators, board members, accreditors, and state-level higher education policymakers at a broad range of institutions. In *The Professoriate Reconsidered: A Study of New Faculty Models*, they write, "A return to a largely tenure-track faculty model is highly unlikely, given current economic realities and the concerns with the tenure-track model and priorities of policymakers, legislators, and academic administrators. Furthermore, the tenure-track faculty model has challenges that have gone unaddressed for decades, such as the incentive system that typically does not reward teaching (for more details see Kezar and Maxey, 2015)" (1). While we may not know what new faculty models will be in the future, research seems to suggest faculty employment in higher education will take diverse forms.

In addition to an increase in part-time faculty, there has also been an increase in the degrees granted by institutions in particular fields, suggesting that additional faculty (regardless of employment track) are needed in order to teach the growing number of students in higher education. *The Condition of Education 2017* report states,

> Postsecondary institutions conferred approximately 1.9 million bachelor's degrees in 2014–15. The number of bachelor's degrees conferred overall increased by 456,000 degrees, or 32 percent, between 2004–05 and 2014–15. The three fields of study in which the most bachelor's degrees were conferred—business, health professions and related programs, and social sciences and history—had increases during this period of 17 percent (from 312,000 to 364,000), 168 percent (from 80,700 to 216,000), and 6 percent (from 157,000 to 167,000), respectively. (US Department 261)

What classes, then, do faculty in our field teach if undergraduate students are increasingly seeking degrees in other fields? Perhaps faculty in our field will find themselves teaching classes related to writing in the health professions and related programs, especially since the report goes on to say, "Of these 20 fields [that the report studied], the field with the smallest percentage increase . . . was English language and literature/letters (17 percent, from 1,200 to 1,400 degrees)" (266). Looking at writing-related fields, and more broadly composition and rhetoric, we can turn to the Modern Language Association's "Report on the MLA *Job Information List*, 2016–2017." The report states the following about the decline in jobs:

> I[n] 2016–17, the decline in the number of jobs advertised in the MLA *Job Information List* (*JIL*) continued for a fifth consecutive year. The JIL's English edition announced 851 jobs, 102 (10.7%) fewer than in 2015–16. . . . The 851 jobs in the English edition for 2016–17 are 249 (22.6%) below the 1,100 advertised in 2009–10, the previous low point. (1)

According to the report, there were a total of 217 job ads for composition and rhetoric for 2016–17; 115 of these ads were for tenure-track positions, 97 were for nontenure track, and five did not specify tenure status (24). Comparing job ads for composition and rhetoric with other writing-related fields reveals composition and rhetoric had the highest number of job ads (24). Technical and business writing, for example, had just 74 (24). If we compare this data with the number of PhDs granted at institutions, we can see there are likely more PhDs seeking full-time teaching positions than there are job listings.

According to *The Condition of Education* 2017 report, "The field with the smallest percentage increase [of doctoral degrees conferred] between 2004–05 and 2014–15 was English language and literature/letters (17 percent, from 1,200 to 1,400 degrees)" (US Department 266). Assuming English language and literature/letters includes degrees in composition and rhetoric, the number of composition and rhetoric doctorate degrees is less than 1,400. But such a number likely remains significantly larger than the 217 jobs available. The resulting reality for composition and rhetoric graduates is an ever-increasing competitive market and, likely, a heightened awareness of the role market materials play in both securing a position and establishing a professional identity aligned with our field's needs and values.

The information above was deduced from the *Job Information List*, which is just one source of composition and rhetoric job postings used in the field. While it may not be exhaustive, the list can be used to demonstrate that the number of doctoral degrees conferred and the number of job openings for assistant professors are far from equivalent. For some time now, our field has situated itself as distinct from literature and other language fields through efforts to expand graduates' employability, yet composition and rhetoric seems to reflect the reality many of us who have recently been on the market are all-too-keenly aware of: there exists a disparity between the positions available and the number of qualified individuals seeking to fill them, a disparity reifying the notion that we should all be grateful for any employment we can find.

HERE'S HOW WE . . . *ATTEMPT TO OBTAIN A JOB*

In the face of such slim employment potential, how do we obtain a job in our field? Some of us were mentored to approach the job market while in graduate school. Most of us, however, didn't learn or appreciate the process of navigating the job market until we were in it. Either way, the process probably went something like this: search job ads, create a CV, gather references, write a statement on pedagogy, write a statement on research, assemble teaching materials (i.e., syllabus and assignment examples), assemble writing samples, search job ads again, prepare for an interview, prepare a research presentation, prepare a teaching demonstration, talk with mentors, talk with fellow job seekers, network at conferences, talk with alumni, fill out applications, send out emails, hope for the best; repeat. In doing all of this, important decisions must be made and questions must be answered: How should I market myself? What skills, experience, and expertise do I highlight? And, how do I then live the professional identity I've presented?

The time and effort required to get a job (sometimes months or years) turns getting a job into a job itself. Take, for instance, one part of the process: searching the job ads. There are several online places to do this, such as the *JIL*, as we looked at earlier. There is also the Academic Jobs Wiki, not to mention *The Chronicle*'s and *Inside Higher Ed*'s online database, as well as databases that focus on specific areas, such as that of the Higher Education Recruitment Consortium. Because job ads are regularly posted, revised, updated, or taken down from any of these sites, regularly monitoring them, as well as devising a way to keep track of the ads responded to and those omitted from viability, is a necessary part of the job-market process.

Not only that, while on the job market, you may find yourself forced into uncomfortable situations that make the process even more off-putting. Take, for example, one scenario that occurs on the job market: you go on the job market and suddenly you are competing not only against graduate students at other universities but also against your fellow classmates within your program. Our research suggests such competition can lead to stress and to a need to navigate a new political dynamic among social circles. This was a particular concern for one of our participants, Sam. Sam pointed out when talking about navigating the politics of graduate school how challenging it is when students apply for the same job ads and how one may get an interview and one may not.

While the above describes what *candidates* do, many others are involved in the job-market process, including hiring committees with new faculty serving on them. The amount of time and energy hiring institutions put forth during a search is overwhelming. The committees often consist of faculty members who have other responsibilities at the time—like teaching, researching, and service—and who are tasked with reading hundreds of applications, making phone calls, setting up interviews, writing interview questions, making preparations and arrangements for campus visits and tours, and so forth, all to hire one candidate.

As researchers, we spent the last few years critically reflecting on what it means to apply for a job in our field, which led us to raise several questions about, among other things, financial costs, time commitments, ethical practices, emotional stress, and so forth for all parties involved. Is it okay that graduate students apply for fifty jobs? Is it okay that they must write a wealth of documents, some of which are variations of each other based on specific job ads? Is it okay that they must travel across the country, sometimes at their own expense, for interviews? Is it okay that hiring committees must read one hundred applications? Is it okay that they must devote days to hiring when also teaching classes, conducting research, serving on other committees, and so forth? While the field is attempting to mitigate some of these issues (many hiring committees are opting for phone and video conference calls in lieu of pricey conference interviews, for example), many continue traditional practices.

Caroline Dadas's study of narratives about the job market includes perhaps some of the best examples of how the job market can be less than ideal. In her *CCC*'s article, she provides a thorough look at the locations of the job market, including those that may lend themselves to being exclusive rather than inclusive. She uses narratives to "identify instances of unfair practices" and to examine those locations that "bring to bear social dynamics that significantly affect the actors involved" (68). She also writes that "by maintaining that the job market is 'just hard,' . . . we are providing a refuge for inequitable behavior: that poor candidate treatment should be shrugged off as a typical hardship of the job search" (69). So, what does this mean for you as a graduate student who will eventually go on the job market? It means you do not have to be a passive participant and accept the way things are. More on this in a moment.

All these things, from keeping track of job applications to competing against others, contribute to a process that seems too cumbersome and, as a result, a bit impersonal or even inhumane. Research in our field seems to support this view. For example, in her study on the affective experience and emotional labor of candidates on the academic job market, Jennifer Sano-Franchini writes that the job search should be considered as "an embodied and rhetorical endeavor that is intimately and institutionally situated" (101). She goes on to write that "the job search process, particularly in the early stages, dehumanizes applicants as a way of managing the paperwork as well as committee members' intellectual labor of sifting through applications in a time when they are already reportedly overworked" (108–109).

We considered how much easier it would be for everyone involved in the hiring process if a job seeker could upload a universal application, as well as their materials (CV, cover letter, teaching philosophy, etc.), to an efficient and widely used central online database that potential hiring institutions could log into and search for specific qualifications. Currently, the process works opposite of this, with most job seekers in our field creating an online account for every institution they apply to, filling out the online application for every institution, and then logging back into each institution's system every time they need an update on their application's status. The amount of time doing this seems unnecessary, especially given this same system might be the one and only place institutions post their job ads.

We also wondered whether the resources available to you as a job seeker are adequate and effective in preparing you for the job market. Are graduate school textbooks helpful? Are they misleading? Are faculty mentors doing enough to prepare graduate students for the job market? Are they doing so with the students' best interests in mind or with the school's best interests in mind, or both? Is preparation a responsibility of graduate programs at all? Is it a responsibility of an institution like NCTE? Or the responsibility of such institutions and graduate programs? Although we mentioned earlier that 78.3% of survey participants either *agreed somewhat* or *strongly agreed* that faculty helped them "develop an effective strategy for the job search," seeking out field-based resources beyond faculty mentorship and guidance can offer the supplemental support needed to survive the job-market experience. Currently, the CCCC's Committee on the Status of Graduate Students supports graduate students and offers resources to help with the job market (for specific support, see their blog at http://www.4csogs .org/). In their 2014 report, the committee made the following observations about graduate students and the job market: "The academic job market is a mystifying process for graduate students, they often lack mentorship at their institutions, and CCCC could provide opportunities to assist graduate students in understanding and navigating the job market" (Committee 30). Other institutions have attempted to help new faculty as well. For example, *The Chronicle of Higher Education*'s *New to the Faculty* claims to help make the transition easier, telling readers what to do and not to do during the first week on the job, what to expect during orientation, how to handle themselves in the classroom, and many other strategies and expectations. While such a directive approach can be useful to some, many academics on the market need individualized guidance to navigate the unique situations presented by the interview process and the new-hire experience.

We also wondered about the institutional responsibilities that make the job market what it is. We agree with Sano-Franchini that there is no easy solution to the problems that exist with the job market. Feelings of stress, trauma, alienation, and the like should not be normalized and accepted as part of the job-market process: "There is a problem when, instead of critiquing our institutional practices, the quick fix seems to be to provide a lot of advice, directives, and tips for candidates to navigate—indeed, to survive—the job search, and the problems of the job market are dismissed as the result of larger political and economic issues" (119). Indeed, challenges with the job market are far reaching and occur on many levels within many institutions. Offering up any comprehensive solutions to the problems graduate students (as well as others involved in the job market) face is beyond the scope of this book. However, we hope what we do offer here contributes to your overall sense of preparedness and to the existing and future scholarship on the job market in our field. We support Mendenhall's argument that

> we need to attend to job market forces and institutional structures, in addition to promoting equitable labor solutions, if we want to improve the conditions of academic labor and prepare graduate students to enter the job market successfully. To that end, institutional and disciplinary histories can play a pivotal

role in forwarding equitable and sustainable labor structures for composition. At the very least, such histories can help us navigate our multiple roles, see options for the future, and articulate questions we might ask about how to improve the work lives of those around us. (28)

Reviewing the histories of the job market and job-market ads serves as a way of revealing and confronting the inequities and challenges present in our current model. We add to this that research incorporating contemporary experience into historical trends is needed to understand not only the state of the market but also the potential shape it is taking as our field moves forward. Moreover, integrating this information into both graduate and new-hire professional development potentially assuages concerns about some of the more onerous elements of the process.

To help us see this wide variety of positions, we need more studies on new faculty and on how graduate programs best prepare them. Our study is but one study, and we recognize its shortcomings. Our study, for example, doesn't include those who took on contingent or part-time positions. We only concentrated on full-time assistant professor positions at a variety of institutions. There are certainly positions other than full-time assistant professor positions inside and outside academia that someone might obtain once they graduate from a composition and rhetoric graduate program.

Often, those on the job market apply for a position that garners close to one hundred applicants. Landing a job then becomes a long, arduous process for many, and considering other jobs besides tenure-track positions (like contingent-faculty positions) becomes a necessity. In our study and the research associated with it, we saw very little awareness of the reality that many of us may have to become contingent faculty if we fail to secure full-time positions once we graduate. Very little scholarship emphasizes a need to examine more closely part-time faculty's contribution to our field, and even though this demographic was outside of the scope of our research, we were surprised—perhaps naïvely—that such a vital aspect of our teaching workforce has been left out of the conversation, particularly in graduate programs. Bailey, one of our interview participants, called this lack to our attention when he discussed the culture of the institution in terms of faculty labor, which undeniably includes part-time faculty.

> [My institution has] this really rare situation in that, because we're so affordable for the area, a lot of people apply to us. We're in this situation where we're not worrying about declining enrollment so that part of the institutional culture is really interesting. I think we have three part-time adjunct faculty in an almost eighty-person English department. We have some adjunct faculty who are on long-term contracts; they're year-to-year contracts but they renew and they get evaluated just like everyone else in the union, and they're members of our union. We advocated for our contingent-faculty members. That has really altered my sense of academic labor. I had a sort of felt sense towards adjunct solidarity, but this has also [taught] me some solid ways that work can be done at an institutional level.

The truth is that the full-time professor position is coveted, and we are taught from the earliest days of graduate education that faculty should be grateful for their jobs. Katerina Bodovski observes,

> Many of us are socialized into this trait of academic culture. This is how things are done, goes the unwritten agreement. We prepare our doctoral students for that culture and advise junior faculty members on the job accordingly: This is how the institution works, and you'd better get ready for it. Nobody questions that culture. If you are too weak for the challenge, go elsewhere, find a different occupation.

This attitude is prevalent within the academy and echoed in public perceptions of it. More important, this stance reifies prescribed expectations of faculty professional identity.

In their 2014 report, the Committee on the Status of Graduate Students writes that "nonacademic job prospects are becoming increasingly important to graduate students in our field" (24). They go on to say that "those who expressed this desire for assistance in the nonacademic job search often expressed that there was little support at their institution because their graduate programs often emphasized academic job preparation" (25). This lack was consistent with our findings, as many of our participants talked about how they wished their graduate programs had showed them other possibilities for careers outside academia. Bailey's words summarize this best: "I think that graduate programs can do a better job of helping students to see the vast array of professional identities that end up being available in the field."

Earlier in the chapter, we mention Mendenhall's reason for preparing graduate students for jobs in other areas. Another reason might be the state of the job market itself. Given the numbers we share in this chapter, given that our job market has been framed as a place of survival and that it is increasingly dismal, why not show graduate students other possibilities, other job markets?

Because our research invited participants to think about their graduate school experiences and their experiences during their first years of employment, we were able to get a sense of what happens when someone finally lands a job. We specifically asked participants who were employed as full-time faculty what they wished they had learned in their doctoral programs that would have prepared them for the positions they were in. Many of the participants told us they wished they had been better prepared to handle changes in job responsibilities. Several participants talked about how the job they accepted had changed within the first few years of employment. They talked about how they had been hired to do one thing, and once on the job, found out they would be responsible for another. Kai provides an example of this.

> I wish that my program would have focused more on . . . the reality of being a tenure-track faculty member and more of the politics that come into play because I was thrust into a position where, as soon as I was brought on board, the university increase[d] its rate from an R2 to an R1 and we had a new university president who really denied a lot of tenure cases . . . over the last two years. And when I was brought on board, all of a sudden, I was put into this situation where there was a high degree of politics that were occurring at my university and I really was

> not equip[ped] to figure out how to negotiate or figure out how
> I was going to deal with this reality that the expectations that the
> department had in place for me as a tenure-track faculty mem-
> ber were being ramped up and how was I going to cope with that.

Talk of navigating politics came up quite a bit throughout the
interviews, so much so that we felt compelled to speak more
about this in many of the chapters that follow. But teaching
doctoral students to navigate politics was only one of many suggestions participants had for graduate programs as they prepare
students for the job market and beyond. As our findings reveal,
graduate programs could do a better job at preparing you for
the realities of a faculty position in the field of writing.

They also reveal that hiring institutions could do better in
their hiring processes. However, we believe one reason current
hiring processes in our field have not been revised in significant
ways may be in part due to job satisfaction. Even though participants pointed out the difficulties with the job market, and some
wished they had been better prepared, 80.1% of our participants reported they were overall either *satisfied* or *very satisfied*
with their jobs. Perhaps this satisfaction prevents faculty from
wanting to make significant changes to the processes, despite
the experience they may have had in preparing for and experiencing the job market.

As mentioned, participants in our study stated they wished
their graduate programs had focused not just on preparing
them for full-time faculty positions at R1 institutions but also on
preparing them for the wide variety of jobs accessible to composition and rhetoric PhDs. Given the data above on the number
of PhDs being granted and the fact that there are likely more
PhDs seeking full-time positions at R1 institutions than there
are jobs, other job options have become a necessity for graduate students. It is not surprising that graduate students who are
on the job market for a full-time position at an R1 institution
find the whole process to be a frustrating one. As the participant
at our workshop from the beginning of this chapter demonstrates, applying to thirty jobs and not getting an offer for one of
those is disheartening, to say the least. The job market is telling

our field that when it comes to preparing graduate students for life beyond their PhD programs, we need to encourage students to look at a variety of options besides full-time faculty positions at R1 institutions.

To help prepare you, our graduate students, to become new faculty, there exist a number of field-specific resources— such as the position statements of the WPA council, NCTE, and CCCC—that can be used effectively to advocate for the various kinds of work you will undoubtedly do. The CCCC's "Statement of Professional Guidance for New Faculty Members" for example, aims to prepare graduates on the job market to ask effective and useful questions of their interviewing institutions and departments (https://cccc.ncte.org/cccc/resources/positions/professionalguidance). The Conference on College Composition and Communication's "Scholarship in Rhetoric, Writing, and Communication: Guidelines for Faculty, Deans, and Chairs" and the Council of Writing Program Administrators' "Evaluating the Intellectual Work of Writing Program Administration" can be useful resources for new faculty to provide to hiring departments not expressly familiar with our field or chaired by members of it (Hult and the Portland Resolution Committee). Moreover, specialized statements on work with technology or TESOL can have immeasurable benefits for new faculty struggling to categorize their work in ways institutionally recognizable for contract renewal, tenure, promotion, and so forth. A crucial element that seems lacking in our graduate and new-faculty professional development seems to be demonstrating how these kinds of resources can be used as tools for self-advocacy. Explore the diverse career paths available to you, as well as the ways our field is unique in academia.

HERE ARE QUESTIONS TO CONSIDER . . .
WHEN PUTTING TOGETHER MATERIALS AND CHOOSING THE RIGHT JOB POSITION

In addition to interviewing new faculty about their hiring experience and speaking with faculty at your institution who serve on search committees, we recommend looking to the field for ways to prepare for the job market. As mentioned earlier, organizations like NCTE and CCCC provide several resources and statements that can enable you to think carefully about creating your portfolio of professional documents and searching for a position that is right for you. For example, the "CCCC Statement on Preparing Teachers of College Writing" (Conference in College Composition and Communication) has a section of principles for new and continuing faculty (https:// cccc.ncte.org/cccc/resources/positions/statementonprep). Examine this statement and ones like it in order to answer the following questions:

- How can you use such statements to determine how best to prepare for the job market?
- How can you use such statements to examine your doctoral program's ability to help graduate students become new faculty?
- How can you use such statements to help you write your professional documents?
- How can you use such statements to develop questions to ask during your job interview to find out whether an institution would be the right fit for you and would support you as a new faculty member?

As mentioned, the Modern Language Association's *JIL* has been a primary source of job listings for decades. Within the past ten years or so, however, the field has crowdsourced an Academic Jobs Wiki to share this information for those who cannot move past the *JIL* firewall. We suggest that you visit this wiki at https://academicjobs.wikia.org/wiki/Rhetoric/Compo sition_2021-2022 and locate at least one position that most closely aligns with the kind of work you would like to do after graduate school. Then, consider the following by reflecting on what such a job would mean to you:

- What is it about this position that appeals to you? Professionally? Personally?
- What skills or competencies are specifically requested in the job ad itself?

- Where does your current experience align with these job expectations?
- What opportunities for professional development could help you build these competencies?

HERE ARE MOVES YOU CAN MAKE TO . . .
NETWORK BEFORE YOU ARE ON THE MARKET

Local, regional, and national conferences provide ample opportunities for graduate students to network with others in the field. We recommend not just attending these conferences but also truly participating in them by going to sessions, events, breakfasts, and mentorship opportunities and meeting people from a variety of institutions around the country. Make sure to join special interest groups (SIGs) and committees to meet those who work in your specialization. Learn from them and ask questions of them. To help you, here is an action plan you can use to attend a conference:

Professional-Development Action Plan: Attending a Conference
- Search for calls for proposals (CFPs) and note their due dates.
- Learn more about the theme of the CFPs and determine any overlaps with your research interests. Find out who has written and presented on similar ideas in the past.
- Begin proposal writing, revising, and editing. Work with others who are planning to go, have been to the conferences, and can give you feedback on your writing.
- Make plans for attending, including applying for funding.
- Read the conference program to find out what events, sessions, and SIGs would be best to network at. Also, look for presenters who have similar research interests so you can attend their presentations.
- Meet new people and be sure to follow up with them after the conference in order to build professional relationships.

In addition, as presented in this chapter, several of our colleagues in the field have published and presented on the emotional labor of the job-market experience. In order to better understand the experience of applying for academic jobs from the point of view of the applicant, you can do some research: Locate one of the works discussed in this chapter in terms of the job market and read it to further explore the themes we address here. Then, contact a colleague who is new to the professoriate and ask them about their experience on the job market. Prepare specific questions based on the themes in this chapter and your additional research. Finally, take a moment and reflect on what you learned in doing so.

Strategy 3
DEFINE YOUR TETRAD
TRSA

HERE'S A STORY ABOUT . . . *WHAT A NEW FACULTY MEMBER HAD TO SAY ABOUT THE TETRAD*

On a February day in 2017, Claire and Juliette met in Claire's office to conduct a phone interview with one of the study's selected survey participants. This would be the fourth interview of ten planned for the month, the first of two that day. Molly was traveling for a conference, so she was not available to help with the interviews that day. When the recording device was set and Juliette had her pen and notes ready to go, Claire picked up the phone and dialed Sam, a new faculty member at a public, two-year institution in the Midwest. After introductions and after Claire explained the purpose of the study and that the data from the phone interview that day would be kept confidential according to IRB protocol, Claire began the questioning. Throughout the interview, time and again, Sam reflected on her teaching, research, and service at her college.

> CLAIRE: How do you interpret or understand the concept of professional identity?
>
> SAM: Well, when I think of professional identity, I think of my education, and becoming enculturated in a discipline by people who are doing what I want to do, and learning from them and acting as junior faculty under them. When I think about my own professional identity, I think about how things like my teaching and my scholarship and my service to my college and university fit together. I think of that in comparison to some of my friends who worked at different types of institutions than I do and how that might shape their professional identities as well.

https://doi.org/10.7330/9781646421640.c003

For example, at [my college] we're a teaching-focused institution. I teach 4/4, I have to do some scholarship, but it doesn't
have to be as intense as some of my friends at R1 institutes,
where they have to write books in order to get tenure and to
keep their jobs and that kind of thing. I think about how my
professional identity is shaped by the expectations of both my
discipline but also by the particular institution that I work at.

CLAIRE: So now that you're a full-time faculty member, how has
your professional identity changed since graduate school, if
at all?

SAM: When I was in graduate school, you have to be focused
on research, and I remember claiming that as a big part of
my identity, maybe not the biggest part, but definitely when
I was dissertating, that was huge. That was the only thing I
could think about was my dissertation, and trying to find
a job and the research aspect of things. I've shifted more
now . . . thinking about my research as a component of my
professional identity, and my teaching as a component of my
identity, and my service as a component.

I think of everything as a lot more integrated right now, so
the teaching definitely outweighs everything else. The teaching is the big part of my life, but I do research activity now that
informs my teaching or helps me learn something about my
teaching. So a lot of scholarship of teaching and learning. I do
service that helps inform the choices I make in the classroom,
and the choices I make in the classroom help me decide what
types of service I'm interested in.

HERE'S OUR ADVICE ABOUT . . . *DEFINING TRSA*
WHILE TRYING TO WORK AT AN INSTITUTION
THAT IS TRYING TO DEFINE IT FOR YOU

Being a faculty member means dealing with obligations for
teaching, research (which includes scholarship and publishing), and service—what is referred to as the *triad of the profession*, what we refer to as *TRS* in this book. This triad is often
reiterated in new-faculty guidelines, in promotion criteria, in
graduate courses, and in research about faculty. In fact, as Earle
Reybold and Jennifer Alamia write, "Faculty work is commonly
ascribed to three responsibilities—teaching, research, and
service—the proverbial trinity of faculty roles. Inquiry about

faculty work generally presumes this typology and highlights these functions, often in relation to workload, productivity, and/or university type" (108). As a graduate student, you are probably already familiar with these roles—either from your faculty or in the context of discussions of the composition and rhetoric job market. Even our resources from national organizations like NCTE emphasize discussions of these three activities in one way or another. The Conference on College Composition and Communication's "Statement of Professional Guidance," for example, offers general suggestions about embarking on a career in the field. Though it does include a section for writing program administration work, the statement suggests new faculty should consider what is deemed valuable and important to their institutions in terms of TRS.

The teaching-research-service triad is indeed at the heart of what academics do, including in our field. Drawing from Aaron M. Kuntz as well as Peggy A. Ellis, Antonio Gutierrez de Blume and Lori Candela write, "Faculty work life is conceptualized as any activities, situations, or events that faculty members experience in their academic work roles. At the core of work life, they are the daily activities carried out by a faculty member, including teaching, research, and service, all of which are expected activities of a well-rounded faculty member by organizational administrators" (2). While we see from our research that new faculty participate in TRS (though most often T), they also participate in administrative work, and that administrative work does play a role in our duties and in our field's history as a discipline (as an example, three of our interviewees hold official administrator titles, including WPA and writing center director). Indeed, many of you are interested in pursuing administrative work in composition and rhetoric. In their study of graduate students, the Committee on the Status of Graduate Students found that "two-fifths of respondents are interested in some type of administrative work in higher education," including "being a WPA or running a writing center" (9). So, we argue, as many have before, that administrative work (whether official or unofficial) can make up a lot of what we do and, rather than valued as service, it should be its own category (if we are to use categories to begin with—more on this in the next chapter).

Consequently, this chapter proposes that you understand your job in the professoriate will revolve around not the triad but the *tetrad* of teaching, research, service, and administration (what we refer to as *TRSA*). Additionally, you should understand more deeply what that tetrad means to you on an individual, departmental, university, and disciplinary level. We also suggest you be aware that the ways other faculty, administrators, colleagues, institutions, and so forth define TRSA can differ and may or may not support your definitions. Being able to handle such situations and being ready to negotiate those ways of understanding when necessary can put you in better positions to assume the diverse roles you will be asked to take on in the professoriate. Hiring institutions have different expectations than composition and rhetoric graduate programs in terms of TRSA, and as graduate students, you should not only become aware of administrative responsibilities but also seek experiences related to them (more on that in the next chapter).

Many of our interview participants described having teaching loads, requirements for participating in scholarship, responsibilities for serving their departments and universities, and even administrative roles similar to each other (as a reminder of our interviewees' workload, see table 1.1). However, the way their institutions defined and evaluated this teaching, research, service, and administration varied from one institution to the next and from one person to the next. That's because much of how we define what we do has to do with what we value as individuals but also with how that gets negotiated with what our institutions value. Consider your program of study or your career goals; are there tensions between what you are intrinsically motivated to pursue and what will earn you a full-time position in the field? Those tensions exist at every level. For example, institutional policies for promotion, merit, and tenure often determine the *what* of our work as faculty—much as they might for you at the graduate level. This negotiation may be tricky to learn, but we encourage you to try, while you are still in graduate school, by working with faculty and asking about their experiences with such negotiation. You should be enlightened about the often behind-the-scenes acts that faculty participate in when negotiating.

HERE'S WHAT OUR RESEARCH SAYS ABOUT . . . *THE CURRENT STATE OF TRSA FOR NEW FACULTY*

To help readers understand what we mean by negotiation, we would like to present a snapshot of what TRSA is like for current new faculty in our field and how they have had to revise their graduate school definition of the tetrad. The data from the three phrases of our study make clear it is likely new faculty in our field will devote a lot of their time to teaching, will do some research and service, and may hold an administrative position. This tetrad is different from the tetrad of their composition and rhetoric graduate school days.

On the survey, we specifically asked participants to rank the activities of teaching, research, service, and administration in order of significance as communicated by their hiring institution/program. The activity with the most significance was placed at the top of the list. Seventy percent of participants indicated that their hiring institution/program communicated that the activity of teaching was *essential*, followed by research as *very important*, service as *somewhat important*, and administration as *not important*. When we asked participants personally (in other words, on an individual level) how important these activities are and to rank them in the same manner, 71.94% of participants said teaching was *essential* and 25% said it was *very important*.

On the survey and during the interviews, participants individually valued and suggested their institution valued teaching over research, but the professional documents we collected indicated participants prioritized representations of research. In analyzing the cover-letter documents, for instance, we found that the participants ordered their sections and discussions about these four activities most often by listing or discussing research first, followed by teaching, service, and administration, respectively. Only one participant's cover letter reflected a different order: teaching, service, and research. On participants' CVs, research was most often listed or discussed before teaching, service, and administration. One reason for listing and discussing research first could be related to participants' graduate school experiences. When we asked participants to think about their graduate school experience, we asked them to rank the four activities again in order of importance as communicated by their doctoral program in composition and rhetoric or related study. The results indicated that 77.9% believed their doctoral program communicated that research was *essential* (ranked first on the list), followed by teaching, service, and administration. On the survey, we asked participants whether they published during their doctoral program; the majority of participants said *yes* (69%). So, creating professional documents that talk about research first could be a result of being in a program that places emphasis on the importance of research. What is more interesting, however, is that when we analyzed the participants' data on the survey question "What do you do for a living?," participants' responses included the following word frequencies as the three most common:

- teach, teaches, and teaching (used 114 times)
- writing (used 110 times)
- professor, professors (used 101 times)

In their responses to the question, 196 participants only mentioned the word "research" (along with the related word "researcher") 18 times. Furthermore, when we asked them "When you were in your doctoral program, how did you answer the question, 'What do you do (for a living)?,'" the word "research" (along with related word "researcher") was only used 10 times. "Teach" and "teaching" (used 61 times) were the second most frequently used terms. Furthermore, at the beginning of the interviews, when participants introduced themselves, only one out of the ten interview participants used the word "research."

In their discussions about their identity and how it had changed since their graduate school experience, participants talked about how research was a main priority during graduate study in composition and rhetoric. After graduate school, however, this priority changed to teaching, with research occurring on the side—often as informed by their hiring institution as well as their job description. Our interviewees Casey and Tahir provided good examples of the challenges that occur when shifting priorities from research to teaching. Casey, for example, volleyed back and forth between identifying primarily as a scholar or primarily as a pedagogue and found himself shifting priorities in his new role, almost unintentionally, to meet the more time-sensitive demands of teaching:

> I'm a teacher first. And I definitely thought I was going to be a researcher first. And I still pretend like I am. But at the end of the day, my time is all about teaching and service. That part of my identity as writer and as researcher, even as editor of a journal, even though that is extremely time consuming, I don't feel like that is part of my identity right now. And that feels yucky, but it's true. And again, as a grad student I was researcher first.

Similarly, Tahir found herself pulled in many directions, determined to keep scholarship in the equation despite its less-tangible results in the short term:

> When I started the position it really felt like a matter of survival. I [was] prepping the courses and running the technology. All of that easily could've taken up all of my time, and I had been warned that a lot of new faculty members get caught up in the teaching and fail to pursue their research, so I tried to keep a little bit of research going on on the side, which I'm glad I did. I got a publication out of it. . . . But it felt very unnatural to set aside that time because the teaching gigs are so immediate and the research can feel so discouraging when there's not always a clear end result.

At least three interview participants spoke specifically to the challenge of balancing research when their position was primarily informed by their expertise in teaching. You are likely to experience this shift as you begin a full-time position in the field. While research seems to be the first priority of graduate students, and while new faculty still use professional documents that prioritize representations of their research, a big part of the job—as a professional in composition and rhetoric—is going to be teaching; pedagogy is what we are trained for. On the survey, we asked about the kinds of training participants received as new faculty. Overwhelmingly, the most training participants received involved teaching practices and resources. That is, 76% of participants received this kind of training. Only 34% received training on research practices or resources, 29% on service practices or resources, and 27% on administrative practices or resources. At their institutions, participants in our study teach a variety of courses. Mainly, they teach undergraduate courses (94.8%), while some also teach graduate courses (31.6%) and professional-development/training courses (16.3%). The type of courses they teach include some of the following: general education courses, courses required for a major, area-studies courses, interdisciplinary courses, online courses, basic/developmental courses, and first-year seminar courses.

Even though teaching seemed to be a priority for the new composition and rhetoric faculty in our study, service emerged as a responsibility faculty had to take on but one that was not the biggest part of their job. David Perlmutter, one of the authors featured in *New to the Faculty: Everything New Professors Need to Know to Be Successful*, writes that "service is not an optional part of being an assistant professor. The trick is knowing how to do enough without doing too much" ("Service" 20). He suggests one should think ahead while on the job market so as to develop a plan for service before accepting any job offer. He also suggests faculty make sure that they include service on their CVs (22). For the questions on the survey regarding what they do for a living, no respondent used the word *service*. However, one person did use the word "serve" in their response, writing, "I am a college professor who has to teach, serve and do research for my job." In addition, during their introductions in the interviews, no one used *service* or related terms when introducing their current positions. Nor did they lead with *service* in their professional documents. The service section on our participants' CVs almost always came after their publications, teaching, and administration sections (or was lumped in with their administration sections). More often than not, this section was one of the last on the CVs. Only once did a service section come before a publications section on a participant's CV.

Nearly 86% of the survey participants said they were *satisfied* or *very satisfied* with opportunities to engage in service at their job, whereas 13.7% were *marginally satisfied* or *not satisfied* with such opportunities. During the interviews, many of the participants did talk about service in many capacities. And when they talked about service, they talked, for instance, about working collaboratively with others in their departments, with other departments and colleges on their campuses, and also with their local communities. This work was particularly evident in their responses to the question about being an institutional citizen. For example, Rey spoke about her service as an integral part of her identity and how that is tied to her work with others to build a community.

> To me an institutional citizen is multifaceted. So, part of my citizenship is absolutely serving on committees; . . . it is working to solve problems and make the school better, even to try to identify problems that might come across our way later. Part of that institutional citizenship is creating a safe environment for faculty, for staff, and for students. So, my institutional citizenship to me is actually part of my identity because I'm not just here doing my research, but I'm also here working with other people and making arguments for what this place should be.

Perhaps least surprising in terms of the answers we garnered from participants on the survey question "What do you do for a living?" had to do with administrative work. Participants made sure to include this administrative work if they held these titled positions. They used words like "direct," "director," and "administrator" when talking about these positions. The word "direct," as in, "I direct the _____ program," was used five times, the word "director" was used four times, and the word "administrator" (along with the related word "administrators") was only mentioned twice. In their introductions during the interviews, participants also used the words "director" and "coordinator" to indicate their administrative positions. Five of our ten interviewees indicated they currently held administrative positions directing, coordinating, or administering a program, whether that was a writing program or an internship program.

HERE'S WHAT SCHOLARSHIP SAYS ABOUT . . . *ADMINISTRATIVE WORK*

To begin with, we want to point out that our field has made quite a few calls in the last fifteen years to better prepare graduate students for administrative work in the field of composition and rhetoric. We point this out in this chapter on TRSA because teaching and research have been (and still are) much of the focus of graduate programs in our field. While Anthony Edgington and Stacy Hartlage Taylor's work in 2007 notes that "more graduate programs in composition and rhetoric are asking graduate students to work in administrative positions as part of their assistantships" (150), and that while such positions have "led many to a greater sense of what the field of composition and rhetoric truly encompasses" and have "provided a fuller picture of the life they had chosen to lead" (157), graduate programs could do more to ensure such positions adequately prepare these future administrators for what life is really like once on the job. Based on their survey of both WPAs and GSAs, Edgington and Taylor argue that rather than shield GSAs from some of the hard work involved in WPA work, "GSAs should have the opportunity to receive more behind-the-scenes work during their tenure in the position" and that they should be "invited to participate in hiring and firing decisions, allowed to work with the WPA on budgetary issues, and made aware of the political and social forces that define their work" (166). A defining characteristic of our field is that our graduate students not only receive extensive training in teaching but are also afforded opportunities for professional development that prepares them to serve in a leadership capacity at their institutions, representing composition and rhetoric as a field of study defined as much by practice as it is by pedagogy.

Returning to Giberson et al.'s 2009 study, a study we mention earlier in this book, we can find another example of a call for graduate school preparation to better prepare students for the administrative work they will do as junior faculty. Their study examined how junior faculty responded to their new responsibilities of developing an undergraduate writing major. While the authors are encouraged by the fact that "graduate faculty responsible for training future Writing Program Administrators have taken a particular interest in graduate student professionalization, providing graduate courses in administration of first-year composition programs as well as increasing opportunities for graduate assistantships in FYC program administration," they point out that "as the discipline of composition and rhetoric continues to change and evolve, however, so must these efforts to professionalize graduate students to prepare them for emerging disciplinary realities." In fact, in one of the narratives, one author argues that "we lack the intellectual and scholarly material necessary to prepare future faculty for this kind of program building." As you think about this scholarship, you might consider how your own program meets or does not meet such calls for better preparation and how you might develop intellectual and scholarly material that can help in this process.

In addition, it would be a good idea to get a broader sense of some of the trends in the kinds of responsibilities new faculty take on. In 2014, Cristyn L. Elder, Megan Schoen, and Ryan Skinnell's study contended that "[t]he assumption that most composition and rhetoric scholars will have WPA responsibilities or will likely take a turn is lessening as growing numbers of PhDs in composition and rhetoric are minted" (22). The reason, they claim, is that composition and rhetoric PhD graduates "have more options than they once did that do not necessarily include administration, including positions as teachers and researchers at two-year schools, at PhD-granting institutions, and in programs with numerous composition and rhetoric faculty members" (22). However, because in our study there were several new faculty who were serving as WPAs, we want to reiterate that today's new faculty are still expected in some cases to be

WPAs and should be prepared for such positions—particularly at institutions with limited faculty expertise in composition and rhetoric. We argue, as do Elder et al., that we need composition and rhetoric PhD programs to help graduate students specialize in WPA work, though we would add there are other administrative positions they could also specialize in, such as writing center director. We agree with these scholars that course work, while vital, is not enough to prepare new faculty for the realities of such work (14). We, like Elder et al., wish to see the field and its organizations support graduate students in their efforts to prepare for administrative work (26) and hope such support does more to bring experiential learning opportunities to the table, ones not disconnected from "the theory and research of the field" (24).

In addition, we argue that composition and rhetoric graduate students should be better prepared to take on unofficial administrative work, that is, work that doesn't fall under an official title or faculty position. Faculty and graduate students often participate in the work a WPA does when asked to help with creating budgets and curriculum, train adjuncts, lead workshops, create rubrics, and so forth. In their work on preparing graduate students, Foley-Schramm et al. tell the story of how they, as composition and rhetoric graduate students, worked together to create a university-wide writing rubric and the challenges they faced. They contend that when preparing to do such administrative work, graduate students "must be cognizant of complexities which accompany such work" and the "tensions that can arise around issues of ownership, authorship, agency, and exigence," as these can be "far more complicated than even the most illustrative accounts can fully document" (96–97).

HERE'S HOW WE . . . *CAN BETTER SERVE OUR GRADUATE STUDENTS*

Our field's doctoral programs are successful in a number of ways in preparing students to become full-time faculty members. A look at our survey results, as well as the interview transcripts and collected documents, supports this conclusion. For instance, we asked survey participants to reflect on their experiences in their composition and rhetoric doctoral programs and the expectations those doctoral programs set for students. We chose to ask students about such expectations at their graduate institution because we believed such expectations had most likely informed their present expectations for themselves as full-time faculty. The majority of our participants, for example, either *agreed somewhat* or *strongly agreed* that when they were in their doctoral programs, those programs expected them to do the following: "develop expertise in teaching," "compete for research opportunities," "publish before graduation," "engage in service," and "learn about writing program administration." In terms of opportunities to meet such expectations, participants indicated that, more often than not, they had been *satisfied* or *very satisfied* with the opportunities their doctoral programs provided to meet these expectations. They indicated they indeed had opportunities to develop scholarship, improve teaching, engage in service, and take on administrative positions. In fact, when it came to program satisfaction, the majority of participants (96%) were either *satisfied* or *very satisfied* with their doctoral program.

If teaching is both an institutional and disciplinary value, we might assume pedagogical development should continue once a candidate is hired and that their experiences in teaching should continue to develop. Yet, as we found, while 54.5% of the survey participants were *satisfied* or *very satisfied* with opportunities to improve teaching at their job, 45.4% were *marginally satisfied* or *not satisfied* with such opportunities. That nearly half are *marginally satisfied* or *not satisfied* suggests a discrepancy between the values communicated and the values lived within their institutional cultures.

Second, several of our interviewees mentioned that their composition and rhetoric doctoral programs helped prepare them to teach and participate in research. Like other participants, Bailey talked at length about how when planning and teaching his own classes, he draws on his experience in his doctoral program utilizing what he learned about giving feed-back to students and valuing and trusting student work.

In terms of developing professional identity, survey par-ticipants *agreed strongly* that by the final term of their doctoral program, they felt attending conferences, pursuing research subjects that were of interest, and successfully defending a dis-sertation were important for developing professional identity. In addition, overwhelmingly, 134 participants, or 74%, *strongly agreed* they identified as a teacher in their field by the final term of their program. Finally, while our field would probably prefer to see higher percentages, by the time of graduation, a slight majority of participants were *confident* or *very confident* in the following:

- understanding teaching and learning processes (55.8%),
- using technology in education (51.9%),
- communicating appropriately to various audiences (61.3%),
- working in diverse groups (69%),
- and articulating core purposes and values of higher educa-tion (50.2%).

A book on preparing new faculty and providing support would not be complete without talking more specifically about all the responsibilities new faculty take on when they teach, research, serve, and administer. Striking the right balance among these, as the pages of this book argue, is not an easy task nor is it a prior-ity for composition and rhetoric professionals in some cases. But, our graduate programs would do well to teach new faculty to understand the contexts in which this tetrad is enacted by offer-ing more assistance, instruction, and resources. The tetrad is certainly tied to time management in the sense that we manage our time based on what we have to do, and what we have to do is teach, research, serve, and administer. But those tasks are not necessarily all we do, and the degree to which we do these—that is, the time we set aside for these things—can often be depen-dent on a number of factors, the first being negotiating our own expectations with the expectations of our hiring institutions.

As an example, one area graduate schools could improve upon is service. Our survey results indicate that when entering their doctoral programs, only 11% of our participants said they were *very confident* in engaging in service opportunities, while 30.9% of our participants said they were *confident* in engaging in service opportunities. Fifty-eight percent of our participants, however, said they were *neutral, hesitant,* or *very hesitant* about engaging in service opportunities. By the time these participants graduated, confidence levels only slightly changed. At the time of graduation, nearly 29% of participants were *very confident* in engaging in service opportunities, while nearly 43% of participants said they were *confident.* Nearly 29% still said they were *neutral, hesitant,* or *very hesitant* about engaging in service opportunities.

Compared to participants' confidence levels for teaching and research at the beginning and end of their doctoral programs, the confidence levels for service showed less increase. Only 23% of participants said they were *confident* or *very confident* about applying research methods and methodologies at the start of their doctoral program. Those percentages increased significantly to 82.3% by the time of graduation. Likewise, at the start of their programs, nearly 56% of participants said they were *confident* or *very confident* about understanding teaching and learning processes, and nearly 52% said they were *confident* or *very confident* about using technology in education. Those percentages increased significantly by the time of graduation, with nearly 92% of participants saying they were *confident* or *very confident* about understanding teaching and learning processes and 86% saying they were *confident* or *very confident* about using technology in education.

HERE ARE QUESTIONS TO CONSIDER . . . *ABOUT THE MATERIAL REALITIES OF THE TETRAD*

Now that you have had a chance to reflect on the tetrad, we want to offer you a means to discuss your program's role in preparing students for the professoriate, as well as offer up some questions you can use to research your future career path by examining the work you do now. To start, look at your current workload in your program through the lens of the tetrad. Then, answer the following:

- **Teaching**: What opportunities have you been given to teach courses at the college level? Which aspects of our field inform your teaching? Where do you see theory informing practice and practice informing theory in your own experiences of teaching?

- **Research**: Think about an upcoming research project, such as a seminar paper, conference presentation, or draft of a paper for publication. First consider the overarching outcome you hope will result from the research work, and then create a very specific task list that can help you get started:

    - **Planning**: How do you like to get started with a project? Do you make a To-Do list? Do you schedule tasks on your calendar, working backwards from the deadline/due date? What materials and tools do you like to use? (e.g., pen and paper, word processor, Web-based composing, software for project management) What are the tangible steps you would need to take (or that you like to take based on personal preferences) before beginning the data collection? Who can help you with these steps?

    - **Literature Review Research**: How do you begin exploring a topic of interest relevant to the field of composition and rhetoric? Do you utilize your institution's databases? Do you explore first through Google Scholar? Do you use popular repositories of information like Wikipedia to help you frame the scope of your area of interest? Make a specific list of resources you have access to and keep track of search words—and Boolean operator usage—so you can retrace your steps at a later date. In academic research, common words take on different meaning (e.g., the term *public* as used by most people versus Michael Warner's definition of *publics*). Consider creating a table to track works relevant to your scope and avoid the rabbit hole that can sometimes befall our good-intentioned initial research processes. Compare your method of researching with your colleagues' and even your graduate program professors'. Sharing the material tasks of researching can help to better manage one's time and demystify research processes.

Table 3.1. Research Table

Database/ Resource	Keywords	Authors & Title	Relevance

- **Service**: What work do you/could you do outside your assistantship and coursework that might be considered service? Are there opportunities that a composition and rhetoric professional could be considered uniquely prepared to take advantage of? Consider the various levels and contexts of service: program, department, college (disciplinary and/or a graduate school/college), the university, partnerships with academia, and communities outside academia. Is this work valued in the context of your composition and rhetoric graduate program? How about in the context of the department? College? Institution at large? How do you know?

- **Administration**: What official and unofficial administrative work do you do, and how much time do you spend on it? Are you doing too much or too little of this work? What have you learned from this work? What skills have you developed? What more do you want to get out of this work? In what ways do you believe you will be able to transfer the knowledge and skills learned during this work to your future position in the composition and rhetoric professoriate?

HERE ARE MOVES YOU CAN MAKE TO . . . *BECOME MORE PROFICIENT IN ALL AREAS OF THE TETRAD*

Ask composition and rhetoric colleagues who are senior faculty or new to the professoriate whether you can interview them regarding their position. Compose 5–10 questions in which you ask them to explore their expectations prior to being hired versus their current lived experiences as a professor. Be sure to ask specifically about each element of the tetrad: teaching, research, service, and administration.

Ask if you could shadow them in terms of what they do for TRSA as they prepare and teach classes, as they research, as they serve their institutions, departments, and communities, and as they participate in administrative work. If shadowing is not possible, look for other opportunities in and outside your program that will give you experience in TRSA as a composition and rhetoric professional. For example, working in a university writing center could help you get an understanding of service and administrative work, as well as teaching.

Strategy 4
PREPARE FOR MORE THAN TRSA

I just wish that my program would have focused more, at some point . . . on . . . what it's like being an assistant professor.
—Kai, interviewee

HERE'S A STORY ABOUT . . . *MAKING OUR WORK VISIBLE*
Not long after Juliette was hired as an associate professor, she began working with a colleague to develop a service-learning-based literacy initiative that (originally) wasn't tied to a class, wasn't considered part of her service expectation, didn't have a specific research agenda attached to it, and wasn't an administrative task—in other words, it did not fit neatly into the tetrad of teaching, research, service, and administration. The impetus for the program was that she and a colleague saw a need, both in a local community and in their students' experiences. In an effort to meet those needs, they designed a program that would provide additional literacy experience for the community while also fostering pedagogical development for our students. The program was labor and time intensive for both professors and required coordinating a number of resources at two institutions. To the extent possible, our department supported the initiative, as did a regional organization via a small grant to assist with travel costs for our students. For all involved, the literacy program appeared to be a rewarding project.

However, when Juliette began putting together her annual-review documents, she didn't know how to frame this work in a way that would effectively translate it into a specific area of the tetrad for the review committee. She couldn't discuss the project in one specific category without omitting efforts that spoke to others. If she packaged it as service, where in her review

https://doi.org/10.7330/9781646421640.c004

dossier would she discuss the hours spent on pedagogical development with the students or the material documents she and our colleague created with the students? Presenting the literacy initiative as teaching didn't account for the hours she and our colleague spent coordinating travel for the university group to the mentoring site or the time spent developing the grant. Framing it as teaching undermined the service and administrative parts of the work; likewise, framing it as service downplayed the teaching and administrative parts. She felt the time and effort she and our colleague put into the work wouldn't be recognized during review because of the constraints of our institution's expectations for the dossier and the way the tetrad is defined. Additionally, as a new faculty member, she was concerned that poorly framing the project would undermine her review, making it appear that she hadn't performed adequately in the areas of teaching and service.

Because she was still unsure of just what the committee reviewers were looking for in faculty portfolios and how they would weigh this kind of work, she suddenly felt unprepared and began wondering whether her values—those she believed were shared across our field—were perhaps misplaced in the larger scope of our institution. To get a sense of how she might effectively frame the project in her portfolio, she turned to colleagues, administrators, and peers at other institutions, explicitly seeking advice on how to make visible the invisible aspects of the work—the parts that didn't neatly fit into the prescribed categories of the tetrad. The project had been an invaluable professional-development experience for her personally and, in addition to the easily categorized work of the project, she wanted the relationships she had developed locally through the initiative, the ways the students were benefitting from and using their work with the project, and the lessons she learned about program development to be visible in her dossier. Everyone seemed to have a different opinion on how she should approach the project in her documents. Because she was a new professor in her specific institutional context, the advice from those at other institutions was simultaneously helpful and confusing. Her peers' advice was informed by the values and expectations of their institutions, not ours, and she was still learning how to navigate the ideology of our university. Finally, she turned to one of her graduate school mentors and asked how she would frame the project. Her mentor suggested she would introduce it as a whole in the cover letter but then break out the work into pieces, placing those pieces in different categories so reviewers would see how this project spanned the various expectations of the job and would understand how meaningful the unseen experiences were to Juliette's professional development. After following this advice, Juliette felt some of the work still remained invisible but was grateful she finally had a path to framing the project that would allow her to highlight her professional values, and those of our field, within the scope of our institution's ideology.

HERE'S OUR ADVICE ABOUT . . . *TRYING TO MAKE VISIBLE ALL YOU DO*

As professional writers, we are often called upon to help others write, inside our institutions or external to them. We work with all kinds of people—from high schoolers to senior professionals—to help them write various professional documents, such as personal statements, cover letters, portfolios, resumes, and business proposals. In these instances, we are relying on our expertise to help others accomplish goals through writing, document design, delivery, and so on. If you're wondering if this work "counts" when you're looking toward hiring, promotion, or tenure, we believe the answer is yes. Yet because this work often falls outside the traditional definitions of teaching, service, research, and administration, it can easily become invisible. How do we write about this kind of work on a CV? Do we frame it as service to our community? If so, how do we actually translate the added value of this work to our CVs? Do we name names, count how many times, identify it as consulting work, call it volunteerism? How do we present this work in cover letters or philosophy statements? Do we dedicate sections of each of these documents to different kinds of "invisible" work we've done, or do we frame that work globally; and if the latter is our approach, how do we blend all the experiences into a single concept? Working beyond or outside the institutionally-defined TRSA tetrad comes naturally to many of us; however, framing that work in ways understood by our departments, colleges, universities, disciplines, and communities can prove quite difficult.

Trying to talk about, especially in writing, all we do as faculty can be particularly difficult given that what we do doesn't always fit neatly into the four categories of the tetrad. In graduate programs and on the job, we are asked to produce documents that reflect our accomplishments, our work, and we need some way of organizing this information. As faculty members who have been through several review processes, written CVs, and applied for promotions over the years, we are well aware of the difficulties of trying to neatly categorize all the work we do. And we do a lot. As Twale writes, "All stereotypes aside, faculty perform a multiplicity of complicated roles. That list, in no particular order, includes professor/teacher, researcher, advisor, evaluator, committee member and/or chair, quasi-administrator, writer, editor, reader, thesis/dissertation supervisor, curriculum planner, presenter, discussant, author, change agent, intellectual, ethicist, monitor, learner, reviewer, examiner, and gate-keeper" (2). She is right about the multiplicity of roles faculty take on, which is why we believe what Javier Jiménez says about the triad: "But the tripartite notion of a faculty member's job—teaching, research, and service—is quite misleading. There are multiple variables within each one of those categories that demand a great deal of attention, often in unpredictable ways" (14).

As we crafted our study, and as we created our survey and interview questions, there were times we could clearly see that using a tetrad to capture a picture of what life is like for new faculty was inherently limiting. While we considered renaming the triad a tetrad to account for administrative work, we thought about the other work and experience faculty regularly participate in that does not fit neatly into one of four categories. For example, we knew that new faculty were likely involved in professional development, writing grants, giving guest lectures, taking editorial positions, creating community collaborations, and so on and that there were overlaps with the four categories of TRSA to begin with. Does teacher research belong in both the teaching and research categories? Is it possible at one institution to count them in both but not to do so at another institution?

We wondered, too, how many new faculty were doing invisible administrative work. As researchers, we struggled to define the unofficial administrative work and craft survey questions that would yield insightful data. For example, a faculty member who is not officially a program director or coordinator may be tasked with spearheading recruitment efforts, alumni outreach, or developing marketing materials or budgets for technology in their programs. As we were putting together our survey, we found it difficult to put all these tasks into questions that would ask participants to consider the invisible work they do to help us see our field's administrative work as multifaceted and ubiquitous.

We did choose to expand the traditional triad of teaching, research, and service to the tetrad in order to account for administrative responsibilities. Still, as researchers, our concerns about using a term like *tetrad* and only distinguishing four categories of work (when it could be argued we do so much more) led us to question whether or not trying to neatly categorize our work actually benefits anyone. Is this tetrad rooted in our discipline's long history or academia's or both? Do these histories adequately reflect what we do? Do they help us or hurt us when we think about our career goals and how we want to spend our time?

To begin to answer these questions, in this chapter we explore this kind of *othered* work and experiences with the hope that you, and our field, will continue thinking deeply about the advantages of including a more diverse representation of the work we do. We also hope you will think more deeply about what it takes to do such work. That is, what kinds of preparation and resources are needed for new faculty to be successful in doing such work? As graduate students preparing for new faculty positions, it is in your best interest to diligently consider all the work you do, especially that work you find difficult to categorize in just one neat way. This work is still important to the work of the field and the success of your career, department, and institution. Therefore, we encourage you to find ways to make it count in ways that make it visible.

HERE'S OUR RESEARCH ABOUT . . . *THE OTHER THINGS NEW FACULTY DO ON THE JOB*

In addition to what they indicated on our survey, our interview participants revealed to us a number of ways their doctoral programs had tried to prepare them. They talked at length, for example, about how their doctoral programs provided mentors. Dev explained he benefited substantially from working with his advisors, his professors, and his peers, while Casey talked about how helpful it was to attend a conference with her mentor. Casey later noted she even learned what it meant to be a good colleague while in her doctoral program by watching her advisor and other faculty members get along well together.

While our participants acknowledged the successful aspects of their doctoral programs, they also identified areas for improvement. Indeed, when we asked our participants to reflect back on their doctoral programs, both on the survey and in the interviews, they were not shy about identifying specific things that could have been more helpful. It was these things we researchers were most interested in learning more about because they speak to the things we are often least prepared for as faculty. They also point to what we, as senior colleagues and program faculty, can do better to help you, our graduate students. For example, the survey results show that 37.5% of new-faculty participants felt their doctoral program did *not at all* prepare them to "maintain a healthy balance between personal life and professional life," and a similar percentage, 38.5%, said their doctoral program did *not at all* prepare them to "mentor new faculty"—an interesting finding given they were satisfied with the mentoring they received as students. Nearly 50% of participants said that when thinking about how they felt by the final term of their graduate program, they *disagreed strongly* or *disagreed somewhat* with the statement "I identified as an administrator in my field." Finally, our research tells us that for most new faculty, the hardest part of being on the job seems to be learning how to balance, prioritize, and switch seamlessly among the practices of teaching, researching, serving, and administering—responsibilities graduate programs no doubt require of students but fail to adequately prepare them to balance simultaneously when they are actually full-time faculty.

Probably the most telling data we garnered from our study came from participants' responses to the questions, "What do you wish you had learned during your doctoral program that could help you now as a full-time faculty member, and why?" (see table 4.1).

One of the most important skills we learn (or need to learn) in graduate school in composition and rhetoric is how to assert agency over the work we do without jeopardizing burgeoning relationships, advancement, and future opportunities. During the interview, Alex said he wished he had learned to say no to many of the service requests he got as a faculty member. As he explained, "Learning to say no I think would've been really valuable. And not just learning to say no but learning why you should be saying no and learning that you might want to do every project but all that's gonna take away from your time. That's gonna take away from your research." He was not alone in wanting to understand how to choose which opportunities to accept and how to do so in a way that not only benefits professional development but also promotes job satisfaction and individual professional goals.

There were other avenues, too, that interviewees wished their doctoral programs had explored. Sam's doctoral program seemed to privilege a particular type of institution over others, which she found unhelpful because it only illustrated one career path she could take once she graduated. She explained:

Table 4.1. Survey Results: What Do You Wish You Had Learned during Your Doctoral Program . . . ?

Respondents said they wished they had

- had a better sense of how to balance research, teaching, service, and administrative work;

- published more to build their CVs;

- gained experience in creating annual reports of themselves and evaluating practices in order to measure learning outcomes;

- known how time-consuming committee work can be and what committee work really involves;

- learned how to say no, especially to all the service requests they received in their first three years on the job;

- learned how to define themselves as teachers first, scholars second;

- learned to write grants for money and fellowships;

- learned about the field-specific opportunities beyond R1 positions and the professoriate;

- heard from their PhD-program alumni to find out what they did after they graduated;

- established administration skills;

- developed a better understanding of the institutional context within a larger state university system;

- experienced how to negotiate institutional politics;

- become fluent in a foreign language.

I personally would have really benefited from someone saying, "I work at a community college," or "I work at a two-year college," or "teaching is my primary focus, I teach [4/4], I teach [5/5], or [4/5]," or whatever . . . there's many other paths that people can take. I would have liked more exposure to people who were at the type of institution that I ended up in, just to know what their day-to-day life was like and what their expectations were for keeping their jobs and tenure and things like that.

Her explanation of how her doctoral program was lacking in its ability to show its students a variety of career options was not unlike that of other participants. Bailey, for instance, also said he wished his doctoral program had shown students there were more options than just becoming a rigorous researcher once they graduated. He contended, "There wasn't a ton of support for how to be a consummate professional in [our field] and define yourself as a teacher first, scholar second. I think that graduate programs can do a better job of helping students to see the vast array of professional identities that end up being available in the field."

New faculty are often expected to know how to create annual reports of themselves, how to say no, how to establish administration skills, and how to negotiate institutional politics, often without much prior training. When your graduate program supports your professional development in these ways, you begin to experience the work that occurs beyond the tetrad and gain a deeper sense of what to expect as a new faculty member. Moreover, when you are aware of how institutionally specific this work can be, you are better equipped to critically integrate into your hiring institution.

HERE'S WHAT SCHOLARSHIP SAYS ABOUT . . .
RESEARCH I INSTITUTIONS AND OUR FIELD

In *New to the Faculty: Everything New Professors Need to Know to Be Successful*, Brian Brems likens the experience of becoming a new tenure-track faculty member to being in an upside-down ship, the kind in the movie *The Poseidon Adventure* (27). He writes,

> I had been an adjunct for about four years prior to becoming full time. So I thought I knew my way around the docks. I had done the job: teach, meet with students, grade papers, and plan the next day. But then, I got the tenure-track job. Suddenly, up is down. There's a chandelier at my feet. Stairs disappear into the ceiling like the Escher painting. It's the same ship, but everything's different, and what I thought the job was turns out to be just that: the same, but different. (27)

As we were once new faculty, we can relate. Our experiences transitioning out of our graduate programs and into positions as full-time instructors came with challenges. While our university did support our transitions (offering us orientations, mentors, resources, and the like), there were still difficult times learning to adjust to a new job. Our study's participants also faced challenges they were unprepared for when they became new faculty members. The findings of our study suggest such challenges could have been mitigated had their doctoral programs, our field, and hiring institutions taken more active measures in preparing graduate students for the various roles and responsibilities they will take on as new faculty.

Much of the scholarship of the last twenty years on graduate school preparation seems to say the same thing; there are ways graduate programs can and should improve. After our data had been collected, and as our research team worked to analyze and make sense of it, we compared our findings to similar past studies. We had hoped to find results reflecting significant strides in preparing graduate students to take on roles as full-time faculty members. And while our study shows that in some ways graduate programs have made positive strides, we were surprised to find that in other ways they have not. And so, we worked through our analysis, began writing the manuscript of this book, and continued looking at previous scholarship. Ultimately, we were left wondering, Have we, as a discipline, learned from our past? And, if we have, what lessons remain elusive in the field of composition and rhetoric?

Our biggest concern in answering such questions is best reflected in the quote that opens this chapter. As Kai says, at some point during her time in her graduate program, she wished her professors had taught her what life was really like for an assistant professor. Her sentiment and the sentiments of others in our study are, unfortunately, the same sentiments other graduate students have had in the field of composition and rhetoric for decades now. Edgington and Taylor argue, for instance, that graduate students need to be able to see the invisible work administrators do to best prepare for positions like WPA and that GSAs "should have the opportunity to receive more behind-the-scenes work during their tenure in the position," which should include such things as being "invited to participate in hiring and firing decisions, allowed to work with the WPA on budgetary issues, and made aware of the political and social forces that define their work" (166).

More than twenty years ago, Miller et al.'s findings acknowledged students in our field's graduate programs had "far less satisfaction with and far less understanding about the broader professional realm of rhetoric and composition . . . especially regarding professional development issues, job market difficulties, or the transition from graduate school into the professoriate" (397). In other words, "an alarming number of students simply don't seem to know much about the 'future tense' of their lives as rhetoric and composition professionals" (397). In a lot of ways, our study sheds light on these same deficiencies of graduate programs in our field. Graduate programs, disciplinary members, and hiring institutions assume that once you go on the job market, you are well prepared to take on a job once you land it. After all, by the time you do accept that job, you have been professionalized, taken classes, conducted research, and (usually) taught classes of your own. And if you have experienced those academic tasks, surely you must know exactly how to transfer knowledge of them to other contexts. We believe, however, based on our research, that in some very important ways, that is simply not true. Students still have a hard time imagining life after graduation in our field and in academia in general. For decades now, while programs in our field have been successful at preparing students in some ways (through mentoring especially), they have failed students in other ways, namely in preparing students to manage the diverse jobs and roles they will take on.

As we discuss in the previous chapter and this one, graduate schools tend to favor a curriculum that encourages students to strive for an R1 position. One reason for this may have to do with our field's long-standing metaphor of the teacher as scholar. In speaking about the turn to pedagogy in our field, Shari J. Stenberg wrote nearly fifteen years ago in *Professing and Pedagogy* that

> in the traditional professional model, teaching is positioned as the by-product of research, and teacher development is thought to "naturally" follow scholarly development. We take for granted that the dissertation is the culminating experience of

the doctoral process, and that the ability to produce scholarship sanctions one to profess it to others. We rarely question the fact that students' scholarly progress is nurtured and publicly supported through seminars, publishing workshops, and close mentoring from their dissertation chairs, while support for teaching development occurs much less officially, often in spaces marginal to the doctoral curriculum. (33)

Research is the one summative assessment for doctoral programs. Since the majority of our survey respondents teach at non-R1 institutions, perhaps it is time for programs to develop outcomes that more accurately reflect the work their students will be hired to do and how our disciplinary values and practices can positively inform that work. Moreover, perhaps it is time graduate students like you began requesting more interaction with non-R1 practitioners and more exposure to tasks associated with non-R1 and alt-ac jobs.

Academia is a culture all its own, and therefore membership includes discipline and enculturation, beginning in graduate school. We spend significant time being "disciplined" throughout graduate school, learning what "counts" as scholarship, and contributing in a certain disciplinary niche within our field. Our research project confirms that what faculty in our field do is often diverse and far from the idealized R1 position doctoral programs seem to prop up as the ultimate position one should attain. Much less attention is given to the value of academic work within various academic subcultures (i.e., disciplines, departments, colleges, universities, professional organizations, community). As Lisa Ede articulates in *Situating Composition: Composition Studies and the Politics of Location,* "Those who are immersed in the ideologies of disciplinarity know without thinking that the work that really counts in the academy is work that can be identified on a vita as a publication, successful grant proposal, invited lecture, and so on" (163). Ede's focus on scholarly activity is no coincidence. Research results in a tangible, material contribution to the field's body of knowledge, but it is not the only form of contribution. How can we validate excellence and efforts in teaching or service or administrative work? It's safe to say we are taught as graduate students the value of each line on a CV, but do new faculty really understand the range of professional activity that could "count"? And to whom it matters? Are we taught to identify work that doesn't neatly "fit" into a category on our CV and spotlight it in ways that make it matter? The truth is, there are as many unique positions as there are unique scholars—too many to count. Yet as graduate students, rarely are we coached to prioritize the balancing act of responsibilities within our new position or to identify the invisible work we do, but rather we are trained to prioritize when, where, and what we will next publish. The R1 contexts in which we are educated tend to inform our graduate study—perhaps to too great an extent. As Bailey said in her interview,

> Graduate study is sort of like trying to train up stars. You learn to be a member of the discipline in that it's training you up to be ready, if you are so willing, to take that R1 job and to train you up to get you ready for [turning a dissertation] into a book and being ready to think about that second book project as you're thinking about the first one. I think that's pretty stressful.

Perhaps our field operates on the naïve assumption (or perhaps, even, we have tricked ourselves into believing) that graduate programs best prepare graduate students to take on roles as new faculty by readying them for the competitive cultures typical of R1 institutions. Perhaps a research-focused institution is like New York City: "If you can make it there, you can make it anywhere." But, as we have found, that is rarely the case; jobs are scarce in composition. *The Chronicle of Higher Education* reported in 2018 that "between 1995 and 1998, the Modern Language Association listed 532 tenure-track jobs in composition, or 23 percent of the total number of tenure-track jobs. Between 2015 and 2018, the MLA listed only 352 such jobs in composition, but they now make up 28 percent of the hiring in English" (Kramnick). While the report assures readers that writing instruction is perhaps the one stable profession in the larger field of English, our tenure-track-market possibilities are still respectively limited, and that includes those R1 positions.

Moreover, in analyzing the responses of our participants, in the interviews especially, we found their doctoral programs either offered more general rather than specific advice or focused too heavily on the assumption that all students in the program would end up at an R1 institution. These seem like efficient approaches given the fact that it would be nearly impossible for a program to know each institution its graduate students would end up in and all the individual nuances that come with each of these individual contexts. No two institutions are exactly alike, after all. It also seems as if doctoral programs would want their graduate students to end up in R1 institutions because such hires would make their programs look successful, thus helping recruit future students. It makes sense that the schools at which we are educated value research and would therefore value their students being placed in schools that also prioritize research. However, preparing graduate students for the diverse market opportunities that exist beyond R1 seems like an approach our field should have taken several years ago. The longer we continue traditional methods of professionalizing our newest field members like you, the less prepared our field becomes to address the realities facing us once you are a part of the professoriate, professional writing communities, and the corporate world.

HERE'S HOW WE . . . *DEVELOP A DEEPER UNDERSTANDING OF THE JOB*

So, how do you prepare for the everyday activities that will be implicit in your new-faculty workload, especially in light of the diverse expectations and needs of potential hiring institutions? Recently, *The Chronicle of Higher Education* published *New to the Faculty: Everything New Professors Need to Know to Be Successful.* The guide features stories from new faculty who offer general advice about what to expect in the first year of employment as a new faculty member. From encouraging new faculty to check out their classrooms before teaching at the institution for the first time to advising them to find senior faculty allies, the guide provides anecdotes of what to do and what not to do while teaching, researching, and serving your institution. While the publication offers good advice consistent with some of the findings of our study, at less than forty pages, the guide hardly scratches the surface of what new faculty should expect and clearly doesn't include *everything* new faculty need to know to be successful. In fact, what is most notable about the guide is what is missing, particularly in terms of the tetrad.

Admittedly, it might be impossible to develop one guide that covers everything we do. As is evident in our participants' stories, our work is diverse and is influenced by a number of things: location, institution, colleagues, policies, politics, contracts, and the list goes on. Best practices for professional development, then, might include more firsthand accounts from those who work in our field, detailing their day-to-day responsibilities. Reading a wide variety of accounts from those who work in our field offers a better understanding of how our work isn't just relegated to the tetrad and that, in some cases, it might mean faculty have other obligations. While there are certainly similarities among our teaching, our research, our service to our institutions, and our administrative duties, no two positions are exactly alike.

However, one thing you can do is become familiar with various elements of institutional life that will impact your job expectations and potentially create "invisible" work. For example, did you know that enrollment trends are generally down, especially in the humanities? If you didn't, don't worry; there are countless sources ready to remind you. *Inside Higher Ed* reported in 2018 that undergraduate English-degree conferral is down 20% from 2012 (Flaherty). The response to this decline has been for many departments across the country to revise their undergraduate programs, a task requiring committees, research, reports, and so forth. Understanding the enrollment trends of your hiring institution may help you anticipate changes in additional committee work, marketing and recruitment expectations, available professional-funding opportunities, and teaching loads. While some of this work is easily categorized, note there isn't really a place for "marketing and recruitment" in contemporary CV construction. Further, *The Chronicle of Higher Education*'s publication *The Successful President of Tomorrow: The 5 Skills Future Leaders Will Need* highlights the growing trend of universities reinventing themselves every few years in order to keep up with changing student populations and job-market demands. While you may think "But I don't want to be a university president; this doesn't apply to me!," consider the work involved in rebranding, the materials needed to shift pedagogical priorities, the new initiatives you may be called on to create, run, or revise. All of this (and more) will result in both visible and invisible work.

In other words, often, graduate courses are focused on common situations: teaching courses, doing research, or running a program, as opposed to the more nuanced situations faculty might face: developing marketing materials, negotiating a budget, creating student forms, producing annual-review documents, and saying no to committee work. Sometimes, those nuanced situations are briefly considered in your graduate courses, or perhaps a program workshop or an informal cohort get-together. To learn more, however, we encourage you to seek an experiential approach to professionalization, incorporating regular discussions with various faculty and administrators at different kinds of institutions and engaging in activities that expose you to the diverse situations you may face in faculty positions at a variety of institutions. Ask faculty at your institution (and others) about the extradepartmental influencers they engage (such as enrollment, new technology, university branding, recruitment, undergraduate career development, funding, and budget issues). Ask them to host improv workshops that cast scenarios you might not discuss in the classroom (such as the one that opens this chapter). Reach out to program alumni and ask them to chat with your peers about their job-market experience and some of the unexpected aspects of the work they are doing (or ask your department to develop a speaker series that does this). Finally, the following sections are intended to further help you craft effective learning experiences that will illustrate the complexities that reach beyond the TRSA.

Table 4.2. Questions for Reflection

Questions for you and your graduate student peers	Questions for your mentors and faculty
• What kinds of activities do you do that do not fit neatly into these categories: teaching, research, service, or administration? What kind of support do you need to complete that work? What kind of support have you received? What kind of support is still needed? • When composing job-market documents, how do you frame the "invisible" work you do? • What have been some of the more rewarding career and graduate school experiences that aren't found on your CV? How would you frame those experiences for a non-field-specific administrative audience? • Have you learned to say no as a graduate student? If so, how?	• What kinds of activities do you do that do not fit neatly into these categories: teaching, research, service, or administration? What kind of support do you receive to complete that work? What kind of support is still needed? • When composing promotion or annual-review documents, how do you frame the "invisible" work you do? • What have been some of the more rewarding career experiences that aren't found on your CV? • When and how did you learn to say no as a faculty member? Has this impacted your relationships with peers? With administrators? • What advice would you give me if I were hired at a non-R1 institution? • What was the most valuable advice you received as a new faculty member?

HERE ARE QUESTIONS TO CONSIDER . . . *WHEN THINKING MORE DEEPLY ABOUT TRSA*

While answering the questions in table 4.2 for yourself is important to understanding what TRSA means to you, we also suggest you discuss these questions with fellow graduate students, your faculty mentors, and those who oversee your program. They may provide you with perspectives you haven't previously considered and lead you to investigate how you will make visible all you do once in the professoriate.

HERE ARE MOVES YOU CAN MAKE TO . . . *BETTER PREPARE FOR THE WORK YOU WILL DO*

The foremost task you can engage to better prepare for the work you will do is ask your graduate program to host workshops and conversations with new faculty at different kinds of institutions and to craft stronger experiential professional-development opportunities. This will create a community of practice that reaches beyond your graduate department or university and may allow networking possibilities you find beneficial in the future. You will need letters of recommendation for the job market, letters that illustrate you've not only created a strong record in TRSA but also have developed a network outside your institution that makes you stand out among the crowd. Additionally, we suggest the following two activities:

1. **Practice writing reviews of your work.** Our interviewees mentioned they wished they had learned to do this in graduate school, and we believe regularly engaging in this genre as a student, when you have the ability to receive feedback in a low-stakes environment, will ultimately not only help prepare you for your future as faculty but also help you learn to frame the work in our field that is not easily translated to those outside it. This kind of reflection—necessary when we, as faculty, go up for review, promotion, or contract renewal—is aided by the following:

   - keeping a journal of the work you do,
   - regularly updating your CV,
   - keeping teaching materials organized and accessible for dossier compilation,
   - ensuring you have copies of publications, conference presentations, and workshop materials,
   - maintaining proof of professional engagements.

2. **Keep a journal.** Throughout the semester, gather materials from the above list and keep an ongoing journal. Include in your journal not only notes on teaching, research, service, and administrative activities but also on the activities you participate in or projects you complete (or begin) that do not align with TRSA. At the end of the semester, write a review or report that summarizes this work as if you were preparing a review to illustrate your contributions to the field, your graduate department, and your university, as well as how your time was spent and your next steps. Share your semester review with your faculty mentors for feedback and consider how you might further highlight the work that does not align with TRSA.

Strategy 5

RECOGNIZE YOUR TIME IS VALUABLE AND MANAGE IT WELL

HERE'S A STORY ABOUT . . . *ACCOUNTING FOR A FACULTY MEMBER'S TIME*

> I didn't know that I had to do an internal, annual report, where I looked at my teaching evaluations and measured my learning outcomes. And I talk about how great of a person I am, and why you should keep me on as a faculty member. And pay me money. Like, I never knew I had to do all of that work, in addition to publishing. In addition to teaching my classes. In addition to writing those documents.

As we saw with Juliette's story in chapter 4, "Prepare for More Than TRSA," Casey's frustration with tasks like the annual review that fall outside the traditional tetrad—teaching, research, service, and administration—is common. The self-evaluation-report genre itself reflects the nature of faculty work that leads to challenges in time management and prioritization—particularly as acted upon by external factors and pressures within the institution. Annual reviews function as a genre intended to help us to reflect on past performance and forecast future practices as scholars and teachers. The workforce reality is that, more often than not, these documents become less about improving performance and more about self-advocating for position renewal by accounting for (her) time and (the institution's) money well spent. After two years as an assistant professor, Casey got a sense of how the academic culture of her hiring institution impacts her day-to-day work and consistently informs how she manages her time.

https://doi.org/10.7330/9781646421640.c005

HERE'S OUR ADVICE ABOUT . . .
MAKING TIME WORK FOR YOU

Undeniably, there are only so many hours in a week and only so much a new faculty member can accomplish in those hours. Yet, many of our participants felt unprepared to determine how much time they should spend on each part of the tetrad. As we discuss below, some even joked, as Sam did during her interview, about how their faculty policies required them to devote certain percentages of their time to the different aspects of their job (TRSA), but in reality, those percentages are unrealistic, don't add up, and/or simply can't account for what really happens on a daily basis.

It is important, then, for you to see the difference between time management as a graduate student and time management as a faculty member. Managing one's time in graduate school involves a number of unique responsibilities that may or may not be the same responsibilities new faculty contend with. To a large extent—and we are aware it can vary program to program—your roles and responsibilities as a graduate student are inherently limited. Even if considerable opportunities are made to introduce you and other students to the material realities of teaching, research, service, and administration, there most often exist lower teaching loads, protected time (e.g., ten- or twenty-hour assistantship thresholds), and barriers to entry into the inner workings of the institution because there is a perception that graduate students have not yet gained the academic ethos of their senior colleagues, who make up the professoriate. So how can graduate students in composition and rhetoric prepare for a position if they cannot truly experience it beforehand?

HERE'S WHAT OUR RESEARCH SAYS ABOUT . . . *HOW NEW FACULTY SOMETIMES STRUGGLE TO BALANCE WORKLOAD*

For starters, it may be simultaneously comforting and disheartening to know that new faculty indeed struggle to manage their time effectively and that such a challenge is a defining aspect of the transition into full-time employment in academia. This chapter explores how doctoral-program limitations and advantages inform the transition experiences of new faculty, as does the culture of the institution in which they gain employment. Time management across multiple roles and responsibilities is particularly important to emphasize in our graduate programs.

When it comes to managing time, it is perhaps assumed that such a skill begins to develop in graduate school during a time when you are building your credentials by learning to teach while teaching, learning to research while researching, learning to serve while serving, and learning to administer while administering. As we analyzed the professional documents we collected from our participants, we could see that participants, especially in their cover letters, talked at length about their experiences in teaching, researching, serving, and administering and showed how such practices had prepared them for the positions they were applying for. The fact that all our participants spoke to their various roles and responsibilities in their job-market documents reflects an understanding of faculty work as multidimensional. What was not explicitly communicated was whether performance in every role was exceptional and/or how priorities were established by the candidate during graduate study. Instead, emphasis was informed by the values of the institution to which applicants applied (e.g., speaking to teaching or research first).

In fact, in reading candidates' descriptions of the kinds of teaching, researching, serving, and administering that prepared them, search committees, and perhaps even the candidates themselves, assume these candidates know how to manage their time as they do their work in each of these arenas. Put another way, if they can teach, research, serve, and administrate, then they must be able to manage such responsibilities simultaneously, when in fact such skills were most likely developed over a four-year period and under the guidance of a senior-colleague mentor or advisor. No one talked specifically in their cover letter about having time-management skills, but everyone talked separately about programmatic elements that prepared them to teach, research, serve, and/or administer.

During our study, we found one of the foremost challenges in transitioning into a faculty position seemed to be navigating the changing workload expectations—in terms of both capacity and nature of the job responsibility—with the number of hours in a day. As we interviewed the participants in our study, we repeatedly heard them address complications and growing concerns with the time-labor dynamic. Consistently, it seems practices learned in graduate programs are not necessarily applicable to the realities of full-time faculty work in terms of time management.

Faculty, in general, are expected to be good at everything. Disciplinarily, however, we understand that "best practices" and "sustainable practices" are not synonymous and that the idealized practices so many of us cultivate in graduate school often conflict with the reality we face after a successful job-market search. How do faculty find time for service when they are tasked with heavy teaching loads and producing research? How do faculty successfully juggle multiple department, college, and university committees? When do faculty get to sit with their syllabi and reflectively revise them based on student evaluations, the results of assessment, or developments in the field? These are questions we, the authors, never thought to ask when we were in graduate school. Our hope is that you, as graduate students in composition and rhetoric, might gain a better sense of what you don't know about faculty responsibilities through this chapter.

In *Constructing Knowledge*, Sidney Dobrin reminds us that "time and theory mirror each other; time and theory are progressive narratives" (x). While Dobrin is specifically addressing the field's theory-practice challenge of the late 1990s, we find this notion particularly relevant to the contemporary post-market experience. That is, the relationship of reality of time-management practices to the theoretical frames that define such work becomes difficult to reconcile.

Many new faculty find themselves trying to balance the needs of their institution and the expectations of our field with the desire to cultivate an identity that will shape a desired career path. To demonstrate this, we return to the words of one of our interviewees. In her interview, Sam described her workload, a 4/4 that involved some scholarship, in relationship to developing her identity in her career.

> When I think of professional identity, I think of my education, and becoming enculturated in a discipline by people who are doing what I want to do and learning from them and acting as junior faculty under them. When I think about my own professional identity, I think about how things like my teaching and my scholarship and my service to my college and university fit together.

For Sam, and arguably for anyone entering the profession, understanding expectations—both internal and external—plays a crucial role in shaping professional identity in this new position. Moreover, as faculty members ourselves, we realize how much time faculty spend balancing job responsibilities with the time they have available in a day, a week, a semester, and even an academic year.

When considering the role of academic and institutional cultures in the experience of becoming a new faculty member, it is important to observe value systems and daily activities side by side. Academic cultural values are often invisible, visible only when one keenly observes the academy's members' everyday actions, rituals, and practices—and doing so takes an experienced eye. New faculty are learning about their institutions at the same time they are learning about themselves as teachers, scholars, citizens, and leaders. One of our participants, Tahir, was presented with an opportunity to make visible the value of her position when she was drafting her first professional-development report. This act was not solely for the benefit of the university; it became a transformative moment for her.

> I felt kind of unfocused during my first year, very bogged down in work that didn't feel very satisfying or productive. But then when I went to write up my professional-development report, I essentially had to look over everything that I had done and make a case for how it fit in with the categories [of the report template] and helped extend the mission of the department and the

> university and whatnot. And seeing that all on paper was a hugely encouraging experience. I think in the day-to-day it's easy to lose sight of the big picture and easy to lose sight of all the things that you have done that are valuable, and when I met with my dean to talk about it, he said, "You're one of the most productive members of the department." I was so surprised because I thought for sure everyone was looking at me and thinking I was a slacker.

Such moments of accomplishment and success can be fleeting. Moments later, Tahir lamented, "I still feel like I don't entirely understand the terrain of the university and the opportunities there." Tahir's reflections, specifically, highlight the ebb and flow of confidence—in her work, her knowledge, her place in the university—that is so characteristic of the experiences of new faculty members, particularly in their first three years as they are in transition.

One of the reasons we conducted this research was because we both experienced, in our lives, and observed, in our data, that new faculty are typically unprepared to balance their time effectively, given all their new responsibilities. In fact, as we interviewed participants like Sam, we were struck by how often faculty talked about time and how often their thoughts were preoccupied by trying to manage it effectively and in light of the institution's culture. Sam explains,

> We teach 4/4, so obviously the bulk of our work and our time is meant to be spent on that. We actually have policies, and . . . it's documented somewhere that 80% of our time goes to teaching and 20% is supposed to be broken into research and service. They don't really say 10[%] and 10[%], or 15[%] and 5[%] or whatever, but we often joke that really 100% of our time is focused on teaching and then another 50% of our time is focused on, you guys know, it's hard to juggle everything that you're doing. We have it in documentation that 80% of our time is supposed to be focused on in classroom and outside of classroom activities, prep and grading and things of that nature. It does align with how I see myself . . . I think it shapes how I see my professional identity sort of. If I were at a school right now that was 2/2 instead of 4/4, that would shape my professional identity. I think it would be impossible to have it not, but I'm fortunate in that I saw myself as more of a teacher before I really

started to even go into the job market. . . . That was a huge part of my identity then, so I'm fortunate that I came to a place that was able to encourage me to pursue that part of my identity and focus on it as an important thing.

Sam discussed time in terms of job description and assigned-time allocation (employed by a designated teaching institution, teaching four courses a semester, minimal research expectation, etc.). In terms of time management, 20% of Sam's time is "supposed" to be broken into research and service. The reality, rather the "joke" Sam refers to, that many of faculty in composition and rhetoric understand all too well is that the time demarcation applied by the institution to specific job expectations is unrealistic and misleading, if not altogether impossible. Sam's job description prioritizes teaching, and she reflects on this in comparison to colleagues at research institutions who must prioritize intensive research schedules in order to keep or advance in their positions, acknowledging that the institution's identity is intimately connected to our professional identity and worthy of consideration both as we enter our market search and as we begin navigating the expectations of our new position. We share these findings about time and professional identity with our readers, who are primarily graduate students in composition and rhetoric, because the more you can reflect on what they mean for you, we propose, the more prepared you may be when you enter the professoriate yourself. They may even help you with making decisions about the types of institutions you consider during your job search.

And new faculty develop a keen awareness that professional-identity negotiation is necessary for future success. Data from our national survey provided significant phenomenological evidence; all new faculty engage in defining, maintaining, and negotiating professional identity within their first three years of full-time employment. We were pleased, but not surprised, to find that members of our field acknowledge the necessity and advantage of personal and professional growth. Given the significance of disciplinary values during graduate study, we did not know whether or not new faculty would see the institution as influential in their identity development. We were surprised to find, however, that 48.2% of our survey participants agreed with the statement, "I define my professional identity in terms of institutional expectations." In fact, nearly 86% of respondents either *agreed* or *strongly agreed* that "negotiating my professional identity is necessary for current success." Professional-identity negotiation is a part of professionalization in academia; however, we did not anticipate the extent to which new faculty were aware of their negotiating. A significant number of faculty disclosed they had changed their identity "to better fit with [their] colleagues" (39.7%) or "to appease administration" (33.9%). They felt they had navigated politics in a more intentional way, significantly shifting their values in response to the assumed values of the institution. As we moved into the interview phase of the project, however, we learned not all identity negotiations are as dramatic; most occur during everyday decision making, subtly informed by the culture of the institution.

The context of academic culture in shaping participants' identity-construction processes is important to consider, especially in the ways participants perceived their own nexus of multimembership in the contexts of their graduate and hiring institutions. In qualitative research of this nature, however, we could not just ask our participants this question: "How do you see your professional identity being simultaneously informed by the complex nexus of multimembership as a new faculty member—both in your graduate institution and your hiring institution, as well as in academic culture at large and that of the field of composition and rhetoric?" No, that would not do. Instead, we chose to approach this interview section by asking our participants to interpret two concepts: (1) *professional identity* and (2) *institutional citizenship*. From there, participants tended to elaborate on how their membership in the institution's community of practice was negotiated—and how it was informed by the membership in their graduate institution's community of practice, as well as the discipline of composition and rhetoric.

Interview participants primarily defined institutional citizenship as adding value to the institution through their positionality. However, participants also lamented the lack of explicit communication regarding expectations of the position (teaching, research, service, or administration), which instead seemed vague overall. So, what exactly was valued and the ways one could add value were less easy to discern. Some interviewees talked their way into a definition with which they were content, while others confidently articulated how their job allowed them to contribute in ways valued by the institution, the discipline, or the department. Such hesitations and attenuations are no fault of their own; a new faculty member's conception of their role at their hiring institution is a phenomenon informed by the cultural transition from graduate study to academic employment.

New faculty must parse out these often-assumed, but rarely stated, expectations of a faculty member's performance— expectations even senior colleagues at the institution can't always make tangible for them. The values of academic culture are informed by so many varying ideologies that the reality of employment within any organization of higher education is that it is difficult to know just how one contributes to the institution's mission in every role or responsibility. To get a better idea of how they began to understand the values of their new institution, we asked each of our interview participants to describe their hiring institution's culture and explain what it means to be a good citizen within such a culture.

New faculty members often find themselves in situations they didn't experience as graduate students. As a new faculty member, confessing inexperience or turning down an opportunity can prove challenging. Specifically, the time consumed with service and committee work often caused the greatest culture shock as participants transitioned into faculty positions. Rey noted,

> I don't think I realized how time-consuming committee work was going to be. None of my professors talked about that. They talked about how terrible the job market was, . . . they were very honest about that. They talked about publish or perish, so I was prepared for that. They talked about the demand of teaching, so I was prepared for that. But the kind of work that is seemingly

unconnected to what we're studying in graduate school, I was not prepared for that. So when I came in, I was assigned to six committees my first year here. And I really didn't know what to do, how to even make a motion, why [the committee] existed. And I didn't realize also that, you know, part of my evaluation was going to be based on that participation.

Rey addresses a few key concerns graduate students like you can take note of and begin to anticipate. First, most of the committee work faculty members do is more closely related to the needs of our departments and institutions than it is to teaching or research, or any level of disciplinary expertise. The challenge, then, is knowing how to navigate committee work by seeking opportunities to serve that align with our pedagogical and research agendas as well, achieving the ideal symbiotic relationship. One participant, Lee, explained she had been encouraged as a graduate student to seek out service that connected to the work she was doing, and the experiences proved incredibly formative for her. As a new-faculty hire, Lee explained, "I felt really clearly that I needed to keep my eyes open for service opportunities that especially link into my work as the WPA, so I've ended up being on a lot of committees. . . . I've just kept my eyes open and tried to help the university in its goals, but by winding myself into service work that kind of affects the program that I'm directing." Much like Lee's experiences in graduate school, the initiative will be up to you as the student if your program doesn't formalize such experiences—and most do not, as we learned. Expressing teaching and research interests to faculty and leadership who can steer you toward these kinds of linked opportunities is as important as seeking them out on your own.

Second, Rey notes new faculty are frequently left clueless as to the purpose and goals of the committees on which they serve. Particularly if the committee has been active in previous years, establishing purpose and goals can quickly provide the foundation new faculty need in order to effectively—and efficiently—participate. However, not all new faculty find themselves in a position to ask administrators these questions comfortably in the first few years of employment. Our participants shared that finding a faculty-based mentor with experience at the college or university is a good step toward learning to interpret expectations, particularly when it comes to service assignments like committees, the objectives of which are not spelled out in the job description or employee contract. Some of our participants shared that asking how committee assignments will impact annual reviews is a good conversation to have, if possible, as its outcome may shed light on motivations from department administrators. Do they simply need a representative from the college or department? Or is there a particular role or task leadership expects you to play or accomplish?

The third concern Rey establishes points to the role committee work plays in evaluations and annual reviews. In "The Long, Lonely Job of Homo Academicus," John Ziker reflects that "[t]he work of faculty members was more complex than represented in workload policy and annual reporting activities." Annual evaluations rarely, if ever, reflect actual effort in terms of time spent, and this infrequent assessment fails to present meaningful results for faculty to reflect upon in an effort to establish more effective time-management and productivity strategies.

Another issue affecting meaningful engagement with annual evaluations is how to account for differences across the diverse disciplinary and professional identities of faculty members. The institutionally standardized expectations for portfolios and dossiers rarely afford representation for the nuances of individual career navigation offered in the professoriate and often lead to faculty framing these documents as a justification for retaining their position in the coming year. To put it bluntly, research—especially externally funded research that generates income for the university—is the gold standard; very few institutions are exceptions.

Research activity, it is fair to assume, is valued by the majority of higher education institutions in the United States. None of our participants identified their institutions as *not* valuing research activity. What differed, however, was the range of how research is defined by institutions—what counts toward tenure and/or promotion, can be included in an annual evaluation or identified as a publication in one's CV—and the range of identity alignments and conflicts that arise as a result. Jamie spoke about advancement toward tenure: "You don't put anything in [the CV section titled 'Research'] unless it's a publication," cautioned Jamie. "It doesn't get you anything." At his institution, the expectations regarding research are clearer because there is an expectation of published research in order to be promoted and tenured. Not all participants were given such clear tenure expectations, and even when expectations are clear, a faculty member's own professional goals are equally important, which may create a conflict.

Kai's university has a robust professional-development center, investing significant university resources in pedagogical best practices in higher education, and yet she was told early on that if a faculty member wants to be promoted, generating income for the institution is the gold standard—not teaching. For Kai's institution, publications alone are not enough—not unless they come as a result of externally funded projects: "When I came on board, I was explicitly told that as long as I continue my research and I go and get grants, my teaching will not matter—unless I murder a student. It's going to be my research and my ability to go and get money." Kai—who seeks faculty-development teaching certificates—was taken aback by the conflicting messages.

Lee's experience with vague expectations was similar; she had to seek out information on how to add value: "Like many other places, what's written down on paper often seems to be not quite the thing that the school, as a whole, wants. The tenure and promotion research requirements are different across each department. Each department has their own. There's not a very unified [standard]: here's the kind of research, or the amount of research, or the quality of research that the institution expects." Lee described feeling "uneasy" about the lack of communication. Her administrative role already takes some focus from research activity and yet—as we demonstrate in greater detail below—that administrative labor is seen as "service" at her institution. For Lee, having unclear expectations to guide her everyday work makes the values of the institution much less transparent and adds a layer of fog to her internal identity negotiations.

Participants acknowledged that, much like their own identity negotiations, institutions are also always in transition, to some extent. The stage of such a transition, however, is not always made clear at the time of hiring. We named a trend we saw in at least three of our participants' stories "the bait-and-switch." This scenario occurred when participants were hired by R2 (high research activity) institutions with strong records of valuing teaching. Shortly after onboarding, however, the new faculty member saw the university's efforts to obtain R1 (very high research activity) status. Alex lamented, "That conflicts because as someone who's on the tenure track and who's done a lot of reading about how people get tenure, what's important when you get tenure, I see that research really is the primary thing. So, I feel like it conflicts because the expectations on teaching I feel get in the way of me being able to do the kind of research that I need to do to get tenure so that I can then become a better teacher later." This message of prioritizing research until tenured was echoed across interviews. Whether or not participants intended to follow such advice was less unified.

For example, Tahir's research agenda fell lower and lower on her list of priorities once the day-to-day demands of teaching picked up.

> When I started the position, it really felt like a matter of survival . . . prepping the courses and running the technology. All of that easily could've taken up all of my time, and I had been warned that a lot of new faculty members get caught up in the teaching and fail to pursue their research, so I tried to keep a little bit of research going on the side, which I'm glad I did. I got a publication out of it.

The time-work relationship draws on a network of institutional factors that reflect the changing landscape of academia. The academic job of a college professor twenty years ago differed greatly when compared to the jobs and job market in which you will participate—and yet such stereotypes continue to inform (y)our conceptual understanding of academic work. We recall a meeting in which a colleague of ours voiced this awareness, imploring us to expand our understanding, saying, "If you don't think your job as a professor includes recruitment and marketing, think again." Our graduate programs did not prepare us for these kinds of responsibilities, and we are concerned that you and other cohorts of graduate students may end up in a similar situation.

Extended work hours for any faculty member, according to Jerry A. Jacobs and Sarah E. Winslow in "Overworked Faculty: Job Stresses and Family Demands," can be attributed to four factors: (1) the rising cost of higher education that results in more competition; (2) competing priorities (when teaching and research are given equal value, for example); (3) technological changes, including learning-management systems and distance-learning innovations; and finally (4) a rise in part-time faculty to take on the brunt of teaching efforts, leaving full-time faculty to dedicate the majority of their efforts not necessarily to research but rather to service and administrative responsibilities (i.e., lots and lots of meetings). Ziker's data revealed that

> faculty spend a lot of time in meetings and doing service and administrative tasks. Collaborative research and especially teaching appears to take a backseat in faculty meetings. It is harder to count—and to account for—service and administrative duties . . . and it's hard to quantify the impact of these activities or the time spent, but they are exceedingly important for intellectual progress of the larger [academic community].

One of our interview participants shared her attitude about meetings, saying, "I hate meetings. I hate going to meetings. A big part of all of this stuff that I hate is politics. I've taken myself out of those situations" (Casey). Time-consuming meetings are just one example of how time becomes fractured across more and more responsibilities, with faculty unable to devote enough time to any one responsibility in order to do it effectively. Having the ability or the time to have uninterrupted concentration on scholarship, teaching preparation, or administrative duties has

become impossible for many faculty, and junior faculty are especially at risk of losing sight of work/life balance—but no rank is
more at risk than contingent or part-time faculty, who already
accept teaching positions at a negative input/output ratio of
labor and monetary gain. And while our research did not consider this population explicitly, we know that findings about
unfair workload for full-time faculty are bound to be even more
applicable to part-time faculty.

HERE'S WHAT SCHOLARSHIP SAYS ABOUT . . . *WORKLOAD*

How (much) do faculty work? This question emerges across
publications throughout academia in peer-reviewed journals
and trade-type periodicals like *The Chronicle of Higher Education*
and is most often researched in conjunction with institutional
expectations, demonstrating we should not attempt to divorce
our professional identity from the external expectations placed
on us by our institutions. For example, a recent study on faculty
found that the average faculty work week runs just over fifty-four
hours, of which about 38% is spent on teaching-related activities, about 35% on research, and 27% on service (Gutierrez
de Blume and Candela 9). Two other studies had similar findings, with work weeks that ranged from fifty-four hours (Link
et al.) to sixty-one hours (Ziker).

The question we consider here, then, isn't just about how
often we work but also when we work, what kinds of work we're
doing, and how each faculty member works differently. During
our interviews, participants often discussed their struggle to
identify how and when to engage in specific types of activities.
Tahir notably stated, "I felt surprised by the workload as new
faculty member and [I am] still trying to balance that, still hoping that soon I will be good enough at time management that
I can really start making decisions that reflect who I want to be
as a faculty member versus just doing what I have to do to tread
water." Staying afloat in the first few years as a professor can
seem an insurmountable task, whether it's a full-time or contingent faculty position. Cultivating a specific professional identity

during that time adds a new layer to the challenge and often gets set aside in order to adhere to institutional expectations.

Achievement of work/life balance is one goal that motivates arguments for revised faculty workload and time allocation, yet the most persistent and frequent rebuttals to this argument surround the concepts of freedom and flexibility.

> On the positive side, faculty enjoy academia, appreciate flexibility and autonomy in their job, and have a sense of personal growth in their profession; On the downside, although the flexibility allows faculty to address the emerging or changing needs of their families, they seem to struggle in meeting multiple expectations. Faculty suffered from not having enough time, the burden of juggling teaching, research, service and mentoring, and the need to keep an eye on the clock (e.g., for tenure), as well as producing tangible results (i.e., publications). (Beigi 34)

To further complicate these concepts of freedom and flexibility, Bodovski describes the inner conflict experienced when one's work is valued by others and, at the same time, one's plate is already full: "Requests in academe rarely come in the shape of cold demands; they come tightly wrapped in appreciation. Students enjoyed taking my courses, therefore they want me to serve on their graduate committees. Journal editors value my professional opinion, hence the requests to review manuscripts." As scholars in composition and rhetoric, we are keenly aware of how time-consuming writing can be. Moreover, many of us begin training for administrative positions early in our careers, if not while in graduate school, and quickly realize how many of our service, teaching, research, and administrative tasks are writing-centric. To this end, the awareness granted through our expertise more often than not leaves us feeling frustrated rather than empowered. While we advocate for the value of written work in a variety of media and publication venues or for the recognition that crafting multiple letters of recommendation annually takes valuable time and energy, we see those tasks relegated to the "Professional Service" section of a CV, if they are acknowledged at all.

Even in their first few years as professors, our participants have already observed the dualistic nature of the profession that promises autonomy and a flexible work schedule—having the choice also means owning the responsibility of output—a formula that can lead to a boundaryless career. Tahir discussed freedom not so much as a benefit to the professoriate but as a burden.

> All of a sudden, I could propose a project that didn't have anything to do with my dissertation. That's a little bit intimidating to realize you have that freedom. That means I have to think strategically about where I want to put my research resources. I still feel rather unconfident about that. Do I want to be known as a scholar in one particular thing or do I want to just do what seems relevant at the time?

Bodovski echoes this double-edged sword metaphor for faculty's scheduling flexibility and academic freedom: "A tenured professorship has always been [a] dream job. . . . But the benefits of such freedom and flexibility come at the cost of disappearing boundaries between work and life. . . . We live our lives without margin." But one of our reasons for sharing these realities is to implore you, as graduate students, to not die by this sword. We *can* protect ourselves from it with self-advocacy by learning to say no and cultivating a greater understanding of the culture of the hiring institution in which you find yourself.

HERE'S HOW WE . . . *CAN HELP GRADUATE STUDENTS APPROACH DAILY ROUTINES MORE EFFECTIVELY*

There will always be elements of any profession that cannot be predicted. However, we feel the most promising results of our study translate well into considerations for composition and rhetoric graduate students, such as managing time. Rather than wait until you have the responsibilities of a professor, consider the ways you can begin to think differently about your time, its value, and how you feel it is best spent given the goals of your unique career path.

In the interviews, Tahir's story represents what many of our study's participants believed about their new roles as full-time faculty and about how their doctoral programs, in some ways, did not best prepare them for such roles. Before shedding light on Tahir's story, it's worth noting here that participants did reflect that some aspects of the professoriate simply were not learnable in advance, that one must be a new faculty member to figure out things from there.

Nonetheless, "as a grad student," Tahir informed us, she had "a cushy one class a semester teaching schedule," then suddenly as a new faculty member, she was teaching three different classes a semester, the largest number of courses and widest variety of preps she had ever taught. The new responsibility of managing her time differently than she did in graduate school "felt really impossible at the beginning," particularly when she was also trying to get up to speed with her campus's technology, course-management system, policies, and overall institutional culture.

Tahir's experience not only paints a picture of how over-whelming it can feel, as a new faculty member, to balance the various responsibilities (teaching, research, etc.) but also offers an explanation for how research can quickly lose priority—despite it's being the primary priority in graduate study. She went on to say,

> It felt very unnatural to set aside that time because the teaching gigs are so immediate and the research can feel so discouraging when there's not always a clear end result. You can put hours and hours into something that you don't even know will get published, and that's very hard to motivate yourself to do that, particularly when there's those urgent tasks in front of you.

Tahir attempted to juggle multiple responsibilities simultaneously: "I didn't really think of myself as a researcher so much as just trying to survive right away. And unfortunately, by the end of my second year, I still don't feel as though I have a much firmer sense of who I am professionally."

Moving fluidly from one task to another is not solely a cognitive act in terms of intellectual demand; our participants reveal that shifting from one role to another (teacher, scholar, etc.) within a day requires great social and emotional shifting as well—negotiating internal identity while simultaneously navigating external factors, values, and contexts. Tahir concluded by saying, "I don't know if there would have been a way to learn how to navigate that process, but I felt very unprepared for it." Tahir, like many of the other participants, realized once she was in her new faculty role that she had freedom she hadn't had in her doctoral program, and with such freedom came feelings of uncertainty and intimidation, as well as a need or struggle to find a way to manage all her responsibilities. That new freedom involved many new decisions: prioritizing time for research, adapting to a new curriculum, navigating a new department culture, learning university policies, and deciding if/when to accept service opportunities.

Tahir's story and her thoughts about her new role as a faculty often centered on workload. In our research, we found that workload is often not only socially constructed and internalized as a norm of the profession but also affected by a number of external factors, an aspect of academic work that is often a surprise to new faculty members. As an example, a brief look at the texts in our field used in graduate courses shows little regard for the actual realities of new faculty members in terms of how said faculty spend and manage their time. For graduate students preparing to teach, for instance, there are texts with references on how one can manage a class period, a unit, a semester, and so forth, but hardly are those references taking into consideration an instructor's other responsibilities beyond the classroom. Perhaps *The St. Martin's Guide to Teaching Writing* (Glenn and Goldthwaite), now in its seventh edition, could serve as an example. It certainly teaches students about how to prepare for a course, plan activities, and assess student writing, but it doesn't consider the larger contexts in which teaching takes place and how to adjust. How does one teach a 4/4 load while also balancing two service requirements, proposing a conference presentation, advising students, developing new curriculum, responding to emails, and writing letters of recommendation? Where is the myriad scholarship on these aspects of faculty work in addition to teaching, research, and service? How does one balance tenure expectations while learning a new research culture, applying for external funding, mentoring student tutors, and directing a writing center on a shoestring budget? As evidenced by many of the participants in our study, graduate students might have no idea how to answer these questions based solely on their current experiences in their programs.

Likewise, while *First-Year Composition: From Theory to Practice* (Coxwell-Teague and Lunsford), another book used in graduate courses aimed at preparing future instructors, does a thorough job assembling teaching materials from a diverse population of experienced instructors, it would do well to include more context for each of the classes described and provide insight into the lives of the instructors. By this we mean, What other responsibilities do these instructors take on while teaching such courses? How do they manage to teach these courses in addition to teaching others while at the same time participating in committee work, conducting research, publishing scholarship, and so forth? What we aim to demonstrate in using these examples is that such scholarship would be more beneficial to graduate students if it were better contextualized within the entirety of what faculty do and encounter on a daily basis. In other words, instead of talking about teaching in isolation from what faculty do and encounter on a daily basis, why not speak of it as being an integral part within a larger network of labor itself?

HERE ARE QUESTIONS TO CONSIDER . . . *WHEN THINKING ABOUT TIME MANAGEMENT*

1. Time is a social construct. Consider the ways some communities value promptness and others permit a more relaxed agenda. Time in academia is no different. Consider how the academic year provides a structure for our work and which types of work are or aren't permitted to be completed outside that structure. How does time inform each aspect of the tetrad (teaching, research, service, and administrative work) in terms of processes, timelines, and deadlines?

2. As academics, we are all too familiar with the time that never comes—the time we dream will magically appear in our schedules and allow us to write that chapter or revise that syllabus; the time that will allow us to breathe and

reflect, make progress and grow. What are some other ways of reframing this "time that never comes"? What aspects of academic culture feed or diminish this myth? What aspects of our Western culture feed or diminish this myth?

3. Reybold and Alamia's study found that how new faculty conceive of themselves, in terms of identity, may be a significant factor in career success. Do you see yourself as transient or resilient at this point in your career journey? Why? What informs those senses of self that allow you to see your identity in this way?

4. The culture of the hiring institution had direct influence on the experiences of our study's participants as they transitioned into the professoriate. While this experience is something you cannot access from your current position, you can begin to learn about higher education culture in the United States and specifics within your current institution. What is your institution's identity? Does that align with your professional identity in terms of teaching, research, service, and administration?

HERE ARE MOVES YOU CAN MAKE TO . . . *DEVELOP TIME-MANAGEMENT SKILLS IN GRADUATE SCHOOL*

We considered the potential benefits and drawbacks of providing a list of suggestions toward time-management approaches. After our review of existing scholarship and findings from our own study identified and problematized faculty workload and work/life balance, we were quite surprised to find a dearth of literature on strategies for more efficient time allocation or even recognition of the material realities facing faculty, such as scheduling, information and data organization, and moving among workspaces. We found that few sources included practical resources or shared advice for how to address the material constraints facing new faculty and the ideological implications of current faculty workloads. While we acknowledge there is no single approach to effective time management, part of successfully navigating the first few years of cultivating a professional identity is to find ways that allow us to move away from the "treading water" model Tahir discussed and move toward a more curated approach to our daily routines as faculty. There are countless ways to approach time management, and what follows is a set of suggestions we think would benefit graduate students in composition and rhetoric to consider and "try on" in order to facilitate meaningful reflection of how they work best:

1. **Self-Monitoring**: This action can assist in "maintain[ing] focus on continuous self-improvement" (Ziker). Ziker explains that allocation "might not be explainable as a 'zero-sum' game (more time for teaching meant less time for research) although that's how some faculty looked at it." Time is fluid, and management of it must remain flexible and adaptable. Consider the patterns of the work week and the long-term goals desired. Determine what steps you can take to support these goals and most effectively use your time during grad school. What are your someday goals? What are your semester goals? What are your right-now goals?

2. **Reflection and Time Awareness**: Few empirical studies have been conducted on the benefits of reflecting on time specifically. Ignatius Gous and Jennifer Roberts report that "low on the list of priorities when faced by time pressures is reflection about time. Therefore, people lose track of awareness about time pressures. . . . Control over time and workload requires awareness, and this is an aspect that should be supported and advocated" (276). Journaling and blogging can become useful resources in understanding how time management is engaged (or ignored) and understanding personal patterns (Gallego). Keep a time log for one week, denoting how time is organized, prioritized, assigned for certain tasks, and spent. Before you start, consider what you expect to find; it can be like an experiment, so make a hypothesis! After you have completed the log, consider what actually shows up in terms of how you spend your time. Did you see what you expected? Did anything surprise you? What tangible lessons can you take away from this new awareness?

3. **Developing a Support Network**: Teaching and research networks (communities of practice) can increase productivity (Gous and Roberts; Ziker). Nearly all our interview participants discussed the importance of their support networks in helping cultivate their professional identity early in their careers; many acknowledged they carried part of their network from graduate school into their professional positions.

Complete a mentoring brainstorm in which you consider your support system at this point in your journey:

- **Safe Space**: Someone you feel completely safe around; you can share anything with them without fear of judgement or consequence.

- **Professional Development**: People who provide direct support for you in your academic or career goals. Faculty or advisors might be in this area.

- **Emotional Support**: A person who cares about you and your whole person. Your well-being is very important to them.

- **Intellectual Community**: People who share your passion for learning and knowledge.

- **Role Models**: Mentors who, while they may not directly support you, indirectly guide you because they set an example.

- **Accountability for What Matters**: People who help you keep the big picture. They help you act in accordance with your personal values.

- **Access to Opportunities**: Mentors who always have great suggestions for next steps along your personal and/or professional path(s).

- **Sponsorship**: Mentors who take a direct role in your growth, providing job opportunities, bringing you to important events, and even financially supporting your efforts.

- **Substantive Feedback**: A person who takes significant time to help you make it your best work when you have a project you are working on. (Sometimes that project is your own personal growth).

- **Other**: Specific people in your life who provide mentoring in other contexts—spiritual mentoring or physical wellness, for example. Remember, too, that friends can be mentors. A mentor is anyone who actively helps you to be your best self.

4. **Protecting Time**: Perlmutter notes that "assistant professors who help everyone in every way end up hurting their own productivity" ("Teaching" 19). It can feel like an impossible option, but learning to say no, and considering the value of saying yes—not to another's agenda but to your own—can make a substantial difference in the time-work relationship. This advice can be difficult to follow at this stage because we

encourage graduate students to keep an open mind. One way to consider what these productivity priorities might be is to think about your dream job and then work backward. Enlist the help of your professors (or mentors listed in the activity above) to brainstorm the experiences and skills needed to earn your dream job after graduation. If you want to work in digital media studies, for example, consider attending the Digital Media and Composition workshop offered every year at The Ohio State University. If you would like to conduct research on illness narratives in medical rhetorics, which course-related assignments and projects might allow you to start dabbling in that subfield? If you have a dream of running a writing center, learn how to access leadership positions in general to gain experience and see yourself taking on responsibility. If a leadership role is not directly possible now, apply to work in the center to get a sense of how it is operated from the inside. Trust that every step of your journey contains valuable experiences for your future.

5. **Institutional Culture**: As new faculty take action in their first appointment after graduate school and enter a (potentially) charged political environment, it takes time for them to identify the constraints, boundaries, exigencies, and opportunities of this new culture and be able to articulate just how such external factors inform their work as a professor. Thinking about your current institution, answer the following questions:

   - Describe your current institution's perspective on teaching. How do you know this is your institution's perspective? Does this perspective align with your own, as a future professor?

   - Describe your current institution's perspective on research. How do you know this is your institution's perspective? Does this perspective align with your own, as a future professor?

   - Describe your current institution's perspective on service. How do you know this is your institution's perspective? Does this perspective align with your own, as a future professor?

   - Describe your current institution's perspective on administrative work. How do you know this is your institution's perspective? Does this perspective align with your own, as a future professor?

Strategy 6
COLLABORATE

HERE'S A STORY ABOUT . . . *WHY LEARNING TO COLLABORATE IN GRADUATE SCHOOL MATTERS*

On another day on campus in February 2017, the three of us sat together in Claire's office preparing to conduct an interview, this time with Kai, the participant we wrote about in chapter 4, Strategy 4: Prepare for More than TRSA. Kai works at an R1 institution and has a 2/2 course load. Before we called her, we did what we had done prior to Sam's interview, as well as the other interviews. We centered the phone on Claire's desk, reviewed our interview questions and protocols, readied the voice recorder, and checked the participant's information in our contact list. Often before interviews we informally discussed themes we had begun to unpack in our analysis of the survey data, data we had collected prior to conducting any of our interviews. It wasn't unusual for these themes to change or shift as we moved through the second phase of the project, a phase that involved more data collection, this time through interviews. However, at the time, a few of our anecdotal beliefs about collaboration remained relatively stable, even after our initial survey-data analysis. The trends we saw early into this review suggested participants' professional collaborations were not just actions but rather habits created in their doctoral program experiences that helped them continue to identify opportunities to collaborate once they were in the professoriate. The more experience they had in the field, the more opportunity they saw and created. Unknowingly, Kai was about to confirm the significance of this observation.

We determined Claire would take the lead for this interview and Molly and Juliette would take notes as they listened to the

https://doi.org/10.7330/9781646421640.c006

exchange. After a few general framing questions, our interview script moved us into questions about graduate school. Claire briefly explained the transition and began asking Kai about her graduate experience. In our study, we wanted to know what specific experiences, knowledge, and assumptions followed faculty from graduate school into the professoriate. Claire asked Kai whether she could provide a few examples of what she learned during her doctoral program that she was now using as a faculty member.

Across most of the interviews, faculty tended to acknowledge the difficulty of identifying specific things they carried with them from graduate school; Kai was no exception. She began, "Oh my goodness. Let's see. Oh my gosh. I don't know where to start." But then Kai jumped right into describing the importance of collaboration and mentoring in her doctoral program. She explained that as a new professor, she was teaching her first graduate course, "a mix of MA and PhD students," and that this current opportunity was giving her the chance to "apply that [collaboration and mentoring experience] to students" with whom she was working. Offering an example, Kai noted,

> I came from a program where it was very common for not only students to collaborate [with one another] on teaching and research but also faculty and students to do so as well, even in service activities. I am now working on a research article with an undergraduate student. So, I am trying to find ways to continue this notion of working not only with graduate students but with undergraduate students to do research because this particular undergraduate student wants to go on to graduate school. And so, it's a really good opportunity to work on a particular research area with this student. So, I find that, because I came from an environment with a high degree of collaboration, that I'm now finding ways to carry that forward as a faculty member.

Kai then explained she was also working collaboratively with faculty from her department and two others on various grant projects before reiterating, "Collaboration was something strongly emphasized in my graduate program that I'm carrying forward."

HERE'S OUR ADVICE ABOUT . . . *LEARNING TO COLLABORATE AS A GRADUATE STUDENT*

As you learn more about TRSA—teaching, research, service, and administration—and what they mean to you, it would be a good idea to seek out different opportunities for collaboration while in your PhD program when you have the time and the resources to do so responsibly. In other words, we suggest that when the time is right, you actively pursue such opportunities so you can get a better sense of what TRSA means to you in order to better prepare yourself for the professoriate. You cannot wait for collaborative opportunities to be given to you. Sometimes your course work or program may require collaboration on a group project. But often, opportunities for other kinds of collaboration must be actively sought out. And there are all kinds of collaboration beyond a course's group project. You can gain collaborative experience from presenting with others at conferences, from writing a grant with a faculty member, from working with community members in a writing center, or from developing program initiatives with staff.

Furthermore, we believe learning to collaborate is learning to work with a diverse range of people through diverse experiences. Not all collaborative experiences will be the same. Each time you collaborate, you will work for different purposes and with different people. Even if you collaborate with the same people, you will likely grow and so will they over time as you work together. The important thing is learning that the sharing of resources and responsibilities is a practice at the foundation of most institutions of higher education. Becoming aware of your strengths, as well as on areas in which you seek to grow, is key to being a reflective practitioner in our field of composition and rhetoric.

In such learning, you will develop skills related to the skills you need to be an effective colleague, instructor, researcher, community member, and administrator. Such skills include learning to manage a project and your time, and your ability to be accountable to others. Other skills include learning to be responsible for participation, progress, processes, and products.

Working with others will also provide you with different perspectives from your own, ones you may not know otherwise when working alone.

HERE'S OUR RESEARCH ABOUT . . .
COLLABORATION AMONG NEW FACULTY

Each phase of our research substantiated our understanding that faculty participate in many kinds of collaboration. To help ensure we weren't contributing to a grand narrative of collaboration, we needed to be as objective as possible in our data analysis and minimize our biases. We looked at the data from different perspectives to see whether it lined up consistently. When coding and sifting through our data, connecting ideas, and considering the dynamics of collaboration, we looked not only for explicit dialogical markers of collaboration but also for other terms that could help up us identify instances of collaboration, such as "team," "work together," and the prefix "co," as in, "coauthored." These terms proved helpful in visualizing who participated in collaboration, how new faculty collaborate, when they collaborate, and what they collaborate on.

As we compared graduate experience to faculty experience, we looked at data results both within specific experience groups and across them. For example, we considered emerging patterns after isolating participants with various collaborative opportunities in graduate school to see whether their collaborative activity as new faculty indicated established habits or pointed to circumstance, support, or opportunity. From working on projects, to presenting at conferences, to publishing research, to working on committees, some participants collaborate with colleagues at their own institution (as Kai did), as well as at other institutions, and still others collaborate with their students and with people outside academia. In academia, collaboration can take many forms, and over the course of this research project, we saw different examples of the kinds of collaboration new faculty participate in. Kai's interview story is just one example of the kinds of collaboration some of our participants undertake on a regular basis.

In the documents we collected from our interview participants, for instance, new faculty noted the number of ways they engage in collaboration: in their administrative roles, in their research, in their service to their institutions and communities, and in their pedagogy. However, the most collaboration observed in the collected documents had to do with research. Of the CVs we collected, for instance, every participant (100%) indicated they had collaboratively written and published at least one piece of scholarship, from coauthoring book chapters to coauthoring journal articles. One participant even included an introduction to her CV's scholarship section that specifically highlighted her belief in the value of collaboration in scholarship. Our participants' CVs also confirmed that the majority (77.7%) had copresented at conferences as well.

Additionally, based on our own experiences on hiring committees and being on the job market, we expected to see some mention of collaboration regarding research in the cover letters. In applying for a position, as indicated in their cover letters, participants deliberately expressed their beliefs that collaboration is an important part of the work they do, especially when it comes to research and publishing. Discussions of research often took up a significant portion of their cover letters, sometimes spanning multiple paragraphs. In fact, the majority (66.6%) mentioned collaborative research work in their cover letters.

The interviews also provided a means for some of our survey participants to discuss at length their collaboration with others. When we talked with participants about the concept of institutional citizenship, for instance, many interviewees explained how collaboration plays an important role in their efforts to be a good institutional citizen. Bailey, for example, explained, "My work as a teacher . . . is about making connections across disciplinary boundaries, is about working with staff across the institution, faculty, staff to support student success in whatever way that may mean." Bailey felt collaborating with many different people was an important part of being a faculty member and was a marker of his professional identity.

Furthermore, many of our participants discussed collaboration in relation to various identity frames (institutional citizen, researcher, teacher, administrator, etc.). While participants' engagements in collaboration in regard to service, administrative work, and teaching classes wasn't as explicitly stated in their CVs as their collaborative research endeavors, it was a little clearer in their cover letters, as they pointed out how they collaborated with their colleagues and with their communities in serving their institutions and their communities. In addition, when talking about their pedagogical approaches to teaching writing, participants often explained how they created opportunities in their classes for students to collaborate. For instance, Casey wrote in her cover letter that in her classes she provides "a collaborative atmosphere" and stresses that "writing is a social process." These discussions helped us to not only see *what* kinds of collaboration they participated in and with *whom* but also provided us a means for considering the *when* and *how* of collaboration, while work from the field helped elaborate on the *why*.

We hoped our data would provide insight into the ways collaboration is a part of and affects our graduate experiences, how we work and spend our professional time, and the elements of TRSA. At the core of our questions about collaboration was the desire to better understand the dimensionality of collaborative practices among writing faculty, undergraduate and graduate students, interdisciplinary colleagues, and communities. Articulating the diverse representations of collaborative acts and relationships, we believed, would point to its role in how faculty construct professional identity across various aspects of our work and how we project that identity into both academic and nonacademic spheres.

In order to foster conversation on the who, how, what, and when of faculty collaboration, we describe two primary themes related to collaboration within our findings: opportunity and habit. In terms of defining collaboration in the first phase of our study, we came to a conclusion similar to Lunsford and Ede's; collaboration is more than coauthoring or group writing. It reaches beyond the classroom constraints our field has historically placed upon it. With this in mind, we wanted to uncover the various kinds of collaborative acts our field engages, how these acts manifest, and with whom we participate. We carried these concerns into our interviews and the document collection that rounded out our study.

At the time we created the survey in phase 1, we felt inquiry into collaboration would provide us insights into how faculty construct an identity based on what they do and who they do it with. A breadth of research on collaboration exists in our field, so we felt that combining this disciplinary narrative with quantitative data would provide insight into both professional identity and field identity from the perspective of its newer members—graduate students in composition and rhetoric. Furthermore, with our field's growing body of work centered on public-facing composition and community-based writing, we wondered how many new faculty have access to diverse collaborative opportunities. Frank Farmer asserts that "the sheer breadth of composition's public involvement is already quite extensive, encompassing an array of practices that range from public writing classrooms to community literacies, from service-learning pedagogies to the rapidly shifting contexts of new media, from ethnographic studies of writing in public contexts to activist scholarship committed to social change" (139). When it came to *whom* participants collaborated with, we wanted to know whether faculty collaborated not only with students and colleagues but also with others outside academia.

Specifically, we asked participants on the survey whether, since beginning their current positions, they had participated in collaboration with their local communities in research. We found that nearly 29% of participants indicated they engage in this kind of collaboration. In addition to those who identified as collaborating with local communities, approximately 37% of participants acknowledged they have engaged in public discourse about the field or as representatives of the field since acquiring a full-time faculty position. To make such work a priority, even when the first few years can be disorienting, indicates intention on the part of the new faculty. In other words,

New Faculty Collaboration Experience: "With whom did you collaborate to present or publish research?"

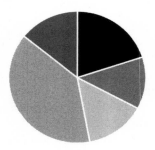

- Undergraduate students   ▪ Graduate students
- Both undergraduate and graduate students   ▪ Neither undergraduate nor graduate students
- Does not apply to current position

Figure 6.1. Survey Results: Faculty Collaboration Experience

they actively sought out such opportunities despite significant demands to dedicate their time to teaching.

While this engagement is not necessarily coauthoring or group writing, providing voice to the discipline in public spaces potentially creates new opportunities for public collaboration and demonstrates our desire to move beyond classrooms and the halls of academe as locations for research and writing.

Moreover, we wanted to know whether new faculty modeled for their students the importance of collaboration with others by creating and engaging with them in collaborative experiences. We asked participants, based on their current positions, "Which students do you collaborate with to present or publish?" We were surprised to find that less than 50% of the faculty surveyed collaborated with students (undergraduates, graduates, and/or both) in their first three years of employment. Almost 20% of participants indicated they collaborate with undergraduate students, 12.8% with graduate students, and 14.3% with both graduate and undergraduate students, while 38.8% indicated neither and 14.3% said this question did not apply to their current position. While we might assume that the 38.8%

of new faculty who indicated they do not collaborate with students simply don't have the time or the resources, given our field's proclivity for such work, we are left to question whether new faculty need additional support for this kind of activity or it simply isn't as urgent as other types of work more commonly prioritized (e.g., tenure requirements) during the early years of professorship.

All this data leads us in a few directions. The first speaks to both individual and institutional identity values and suggests that some, but not all, participants (and their institutions) value community collaboration and/or that mechanisms for community collaboration are already present. While fewer participants than we anticipated reported engaging in this kind of collaboration, we recognize this low number may reflect the degree of institutional support to do this kind of work we receive in our first few years of employment. Moreover, not all institutions recognize the far-reaching impact of public-facing collaboration and may not have the necessary networks and resources to facilitate this particular kind of collaboration. And sometimes those that do provide support possess organizational boundaries that, often unintentionally, discourage collaboration with entities outside the university. A common concern, for example, is the legal risk to representing the university in community work, especially when bringing students off campus, where we are still responsible for their safety but have considerably less control over the spaces they occupy than we do on campus.

The second direction speaks to disciplinary identity and suggests that perhaps our public-facing work isn't as extensive as we conceive it to be. Recognizing that the public turn is relatively young in our field, the grand narrative that has formed around it may be misleading. In subsections of our profession, confirmation bias may have us believe that because we surround ourselves with like-minded colleagues who also do public-facing work, that kind of work appears more prevalent than it really is. While our public work is ever growing, we still have a long way to go to reach the ideals we have situated in our scholarship surrounding this particular collaborative specialization. We see value in thinking about public-facing work, and for more on the growing importance of such work, consider texts such as *After the Public Turn* (Farmer), *Circulation, Writing, and Rhetoric* (Gries and Brooke), *Unruly Rhetorics: Protest, Persuasion, and Publics* (Alexander, Jarrett, and Welch), and *Publics and Counterpublics* (Warner). For dynamic representations of the public turn, see also Laurie Gries's "Writing to Assemble Publics," Nathaniel Rivers's "Geocomposition in Public Rhetoric and Writing Pedagogy," and Deborah Mutnick's "Inscribing the World."

Acknowledging studies of public rhetorics and community research has been a vital turning point in the contemporary casting of our disciplinary identity, but this turn is not the face of the entire field; it is a specialization and may be one not everyone *should* or *can* participate in. Finally, this data may suggest we don't recognize all the public-facing work we do as collaborative. In the brief time the field has been discussing the importance of public-facing work, the very meaning of the term has evolved. No longer is it restricted to counterpublics, subcultures, or marginalized groups; now, public-facing work includes broadcast dialogs and roundtables, Web development, social media, grant writing, and document design. We may not explicitly identify the work we do with students and our community in a service-learning classroom as collaborative; we may not articulate the volunteer work we do locally as collaborative, even if we're writing grants for groups or coordinating their public communication. We may not be able to list it on our CV, but how many friends and family members have we helped with resumes or college-application essays? Not all the work we do outside the university can be easily or cleanly translated into institutionally valued and recognized labor, but as professionally trained writers, do we/can we still consider it collaborative? If it's ingrained into our lives and habits, do we/can we recognize the significance of the collaborative act? The scope of our survey limited our ability to provide a lengthy definition of collaboration, which is a reflection not only of the limitations inherent to surveys as data-collection tools but also of the broad scope of collaboration definitions within the field and among practitioners. A broader understanding of collaboration may help you, as a graduate student, recognize opportunities when they are presented or even reframe work you already do.

But opportunity is only part of the picture. As we mention earlier, we also wanted to know about habits, more specifically about when and where these habits begin. Given that the same participants who collaborate as new faculty also experienced collaboration as graduate students, the data suggest such habits are formed early. We asked participants about their record of collaboration in graduate school that may or may not have carried over into their work life. In our interviews with both Casey and Tahir, for instance, they noted how they draw upon past collaborative experiences in their PhD programs to describe their roles as institutional citizens placing value on collaboration. Casey's experiences with her dissertation advisor and graduate school faculty, for example, led her to believe that part of being a good colleague is to "try to collaborate through publishing opportunities." Tahir echoed this belief when she said, "I did a lot of conference presentations as a grad student, collaboratively and on my own . . . that's something I expect to do throughout my career."

Similarly, Dev, who also has a strong record of collaborative research, discussed the importance of a collaborative approach to pedagogy and course design, noting, "When [nonwriting faculty] put on their course requirements the prerequisite that students need a technical writing course, I want to know what those faculty meant when they made that decision, and I want to make sure the course we're offering is helping them to meet those objectives. That's developing research relationships [. . .] into teaching relationships, and that's developed into a very strong symbiotic relationship between [departments]." Continuing to facilitate collaboration as part of standard practices underscores creating a habitual practice and offers professionals a platform on which to build relationships across disciplinary boundaries.

Nearly 60% of participants said that while in their PhD programs, they collaborated with other graduate students to present or publish, 6.6% said they collaborated with undergraduate

Graduate Student Collaboration Experience: "With whom did you collaborate during your PhD program to present or publish research?"

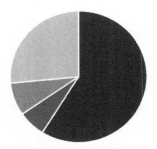

■ Other graduate students   ■ Undergraduate students
■ Both undergraduate and graduate students   ▫ Neither undergraduate nor graduate students

Figure 6.2. Survey Results: Graduate Student Collaboration Experience

students, and 8.2% said they collaborated with both graduate and undergraduate students to present or publish. Almost 27% said they didn't collaborate with graduate or undergraduate students. In terms of collaborating with communities, 26.5% of participants said that, while in their PhD programs, they collaborated with their local communities in research. In comparing survey questions focused on the types of students participants collaborated with when they were in graduate school and who they collaborate with now as faculty, we see that while they were graduate students in their PhD programs, 60% of our participants collaborated with other graduate students to present or publish. But, as faculty members, this relationship diminished somewhat significantly (to 46.5%). In other words, as new faculty, they were not as likely to collaborate with students—graduate or undergraduate—in their first three years of employment.

We wanted to know whether, in addition to collaborating with other graduate students while in their PhD programs, our participants collaborated with the faculty in their programs. When asked about their collaboration experiences in graduate

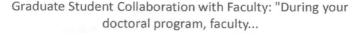

Graduate Student Collaboration with Faculty: "During your
doctoral program, faculty...

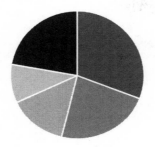

■ Invited you to present at conferences with them ■ Included you in writing a paper for publication

▩ Included you in research grant writing   ▨ All three categories

■ Did not collaborate

Figure 6.3. Survey Results: Graduate Student Collaboration with Faculty

school, 52.5% of participants indicated that faculty in their doctoral program invited them to present at conferences with them, while 39.2% of participants said their faculty included them in writing a paper for publication, and 24.3% of participants said their faculty included them in research-grant writing. Only 16.5% of participants collaborated with faculty in all three categories. However, 38% indicated they did not collaborate with faculty for conferences, publications, or grants.

So far, we have examined new faculty who had experiences of collaboration in graduate school. As one might conclude, previous experience of collaboration as a graduate student enhances the probability that new faculty will seek collaborative experiences in their new positions. What became very interesting was the responses of survey participants who had no experiences collaborating with faculty during graduate school.

Of the participants without collaborative experiences with faculty in graduate school (i.e., "Did not collaborate" in the above figure), 38.6% have not collaborated with graduate or undergraduate students as new faculty, but 46.5% did indicate they have collaborated with students in their current position.

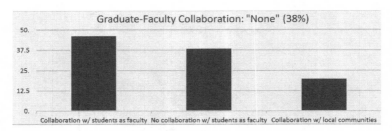

Figure 6.4. Survey Results: Collaboration with Faculty as Graduate Students: "Did not collaborate"

These data indicate that the majority of people without collaborative experience in graduate school are collaborating in their first three years of faculty employment. Additionally, 20% of this same population indicated they collaborate with local communities as faculty. Because this kind of collaboration often must be sought out by the faculty member and does not necessarily align with traditional academic collaborative experiences/relationships, this number is particularly surprising.

In the final stage of examining the dynamics of collaboration, we looked at the 16.5% of our survey population who experienced all levels of collaboration with faculty during their graduate school experience (conferences, publications, and grants; "All" in the Graduate-Faculty Collaboration table). The percentage of those who continue to collaborate with students in their new faculty positions jumps to 73.7%, with only 26.3% indicating they have not worked with students in this kind of endeavor. So, this population is more apt than any other to continue working with students. In other words, graduate students that collaborate with faculty in presenting at conferences and writing publications and grants are more likely to go on to collaborate with students as faculty themselves. Moreover, of the 16.5% who were afforded or sought out diverse collaborative experiences as graduate students, 63.2% continue to collaborate with their local communities. The data trends suggest that participating in collaborative practices early during your graduate study may indicate a greater level of engagement once in the

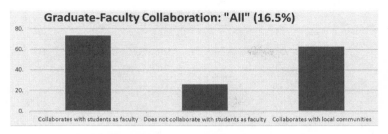

Figure 6.5. Survey Results: Collaboration with Faculty as Graduate Students: "All"

professoriate. It is important to note that the inverse, however, did not present in the data; a lack of opportunity to collaborate in graduate school did not necessarily preclude scholars from collaborating once hired into the professoriate. So, if you haven't had many opportunities to collaborate thus far, seek them out moving forward, whether you continue to study or will start a full-time position in the near future.

According to the specific data discussed in this chapter, the level of satisfaction with and preparedness to collaborate seem to correlate to the opportunities the participants had in graduate school. That is, of the 38% who were not engaged collaboratively in graduate school, approximately 2% disagreed with the statement, "Faculty in my doctoral program were effective teachers," and 26% disagreed with the statement, "Faculty in my doctoral program were effective mentors." To offer perspective on the degree to which collaborative experience is integral to professional development, only 27.2% of these participants indicated they were prepared to collaborate on research when they left their programs. Conversely, those with dynamic collaborative experience in graduate school generally felt more confident in their professors as teachers (nearly 92%) and mentors (nearly 87%), and over 90% expressed confidence in their ability to collaborate as researchers. While program efficacy is not entirely tied to collaboration, our data indicate it plays a significant role in professional development; those graduate students who studied in programs that encourage collaboration, particularly through faculty-student relationships, appear to collaborate with their own students once they become full-time faculty. But this correlation is not causation; new faculty in particular may be tasked with tenure-specific goals, or their hiring institution may not provide the same cultural context for collaboration because of either population differences or internal organizational limitations.

The numbers suggest to us that while faculty in their PhD programs often invited them to collaborate on specific types of work, our study's participants, now faculty themselves, do not participate in as much collaboration with their students. This could be due to a number of factors. However, we posit that creating a culture of collaborative work necessarily involves collaborating more explicitly with our students on all levels. For instance, not all participants in our survey teach at doctoral-granting institutions and may not teach graduate students at all. Only 62 out of the 196 participants (31.6%) who answered the question about what courses they teach indicated they primarily teach graduate courses. Likewise, not all participants are in research positions—as the faculty who taught in their PhD programs most likely were—and therefore might not have the desire or time to collaborate with students, based on their institution's expectations and their institutional responsibilities.

Overall, however, our findings are relatively hopeful. Faculty generally reported they felt prepared to collaborate as they exited their PhD programs. One of the final survey questions asked participants to rate how well their doctoral programs prepared students to collaborate with others on research, on teaching, on service projects, and on administrative tasks. Only 19.8% indicated their programs did not at all prepare them to collaborate on research, while only 18.2% indicated their programs did not at all prepare them to collaborate on teaching. Only 29.3% indicated their programs did not at all prepare them to collaborate on service projects, and 31.5% indicated their programs did not at all prepare them to collaborate on administrative tasks. In other words, more participants than not felt prepared for collaborating in all categories of the tetrad—teaching, research, service, and administration. It is not surprising, though, that more participants indicated no preparation for collaboration in service projects and administrative tasks given the emphasis on research and teaching that many participants felt their programs had and that are most visible in the discourses of composition and rhetoric.

Like most research endeavors, this project's conclusions led to a series of questions worthy of additional study, such as, Do varied types of exposure to collaboration impact the probability that a practitioner will develop collaborative composing habits, and do cross-disciplinary or multicontext collaborative experiences create a stronger propensity for collaboration? Our data strongly suggest that collaborative habits initiated in graduate school will become collaborative habits in faculty positions, yet (and perhaps more interestingly) graduate students *without* collaborative experience still reported collaborating on teaching, research, and public-facing work as faculty. This finding leaves us questioning how practitioners without collaborative experience in graduate school develop collaborative habits as faculty. Additionally, given the significant percentage of participants with graduate-school collaborative experience, we question how we distinguish between collaboration as professional development and collaboration as (academic) cultural indoctrination. How do we, as a field, identify the kinds of collaboration we value and how do we articulate our collaborative work not only throughout the field but within our institutions as well? Developing a deeper understanding of the dynamics of collaboration will enhance our awareness of both our disciplinary identity and our individual professional identities.

HERE'S WHAT SCHOLARSHIP SAYS ABOUT . . .
DEFINING COLLABORATION

In *Writing Together: Collaboration in Theory and Practice*, Lunsford and Ede's continued research into collaboration—a term they acknowledge as somewhat confusing if not altogether problematic to define—suggests that this activity frequently occurs in various professional fields and that most writers, seemingly regardless of their expertise or academic orientation, participate in collaborative activity at some point (73–74). Kathleen Blake Yancey and Michael Spooner assert that the "all-inclusive" understanding of collaboration diminishes its potency as a specific kind of generative action and emphasizes the "mytholog[ical]" grand narrative our field has written around "collaboration" (50). Lunsford and Ede echo this assertion, conceding there is a spectrum of collaboration, and argue that "it is more important to engage collaboration and collaborative writing as richly complex, situated, and materially embedded practices" than to singularly define it (202). Soon after Lunsford and Ede's publication in 2012, William Duffy suggested that, as a field, we align with this renewed focus on collaborative *practice* and "shift how we talk about the benefits of collaboration, away from whatever textual products it might yield, to the kinds of enhanced perception collaborators foster to negotiate the work of composition" (423). Collectively, these scholars are asking us—both as individuals and as members of the field—to consider the dynamics of our collaborative habits, as well as our actions and products. Mara Holt tells us that historically, collaboration is rich in its diversity of practices, that it answers "to the unstable material and political conditions that open spaces for creative thought and democratic action" (126–127). It is not a secret that the field of composition and rhetoric values a diversity of collaborative practices in and out of the writing classroom. As scholars and practitioners, we not only collaborate with students, colleagues, other disciplines, and communities on research and scholarship in many ways but we also help our students collaborate with one another in our classrooms on assignments and activities in many ways. Our very foundations in social constructivism ensure that the social nature of meaning-making practices is an assumption that underlies the field as a whole. Even as fields that rely on collaborative research discourage coauthored texts for reasons such as tenure and promotion, our field advocates its necessity. As Claire Battershill et al. have said, "Some of the most far-sighted and experimental enactments of collaborative work have come from rhetoric and composition" (53).

Over the years, we have identified numerous benefits for collaborating that have continued to lead us to seek out even more collaborative initiatives. In terms of collaborative practices, we know, among other things, that (1) we can sometimes do more together than on our own because collaboration "allows for the division of intellectual labor," (2) what we learn from working together transfers over to our own individual work, and (3) collaboration provides the opportunities for "rich personal and professional relationships to develop" (Hixson-Bowles and Paz). We also see how collaboration amongst colleagues allows us to "interrogate conventional academic modes of knowledge production while contriving new ones to better fit our intellectual, aesthetic, and temporal needs" (Battershill et al., 55). We see these benefits not just in quantitative studies on faculty but in qualitative ones as well, from surveys to narratives.

The benefits of collaborative practices in our classroom are just as many. For a more recent historical approach to defining collaborative learning and pedagogy, we recommend Mara Holt's *Collaborative Learning as Democratic Practice: A History*, as it traces collaborative learning practices from John Dewey and the beginning of the twentieth century to computer-mediated instruction in more modern times. In her scholarship, she argues that we need to see the effectiveness of collaborative learning as tied to "teachers' goals in using it, and that its practice is not separable from its historical and ideological situation" (3). We must realize the histories and ideologies of our own uses of collaborative strategies in order to be "more deliberate about what we do in our classrooms" (3). Yet, Holt's account is but one story of collaborative learning in our field. One only needs to look at Rebecca Moore Howard's bibliographies ("Collaborative") to find many more stories about the collaboration that takes place in and out of our classrooms.

We were not surprised, then, to find in our study that graduate students who collaborate in their PhD programs go on to collaborate as new faculty. What we were left to wonder, however, was how students learned to collaborate while in their PhD programs. Because we didn't ask specific questions to answer this, we turned to scholarship to find out. Surveys and narrative accounts from both graduate students and faculty in our field, as well as in other fields, provided us good perspectives.

In our field, Edgington and Taylor's 2007 survey of WPAs and GSAs and Foley-Schramm et al.'s 2018 narrative account of graduate work were particularly helpful, as they shined the light on collaborative work as crucial in preparing graduate students for administrative work. Edgington and Taylor contend that graduate students benefit when participating in administrative work as long as (1) that work includes meaningful collaborations both within their department and across their colleges and universities, (2) that work includes opportunities to collaborate on committees and with diverse faculty, and (3) that work is visible to others, such as those in the program and department (166). In discussing what and how they learned from their experience working as graduate students on a collaborative project to create a university-wide writing rubric, Foley-Schramm et al. write that graduate students learn best when their experiences "extend beyond the walls of the classroom context with mentors outlining clear expectations of both their own and student's roles in larger projects" and when they are engaged in "discussions of university politics," since such discussions "will not only help collaborative projects run smoothly, but will also help students as they later transition into productive, competent faculty" (94).

Outside our field, Battershill et al.'s account of their collaborative adventures in constructing a digital humanities project furnishes a useful means to see not only what collaboration looks like for faculty but also how faculty near and far learn to successfully collaborate. In telling their stories of building the Modernist Archives Publishing Project (MAPP), the authors share a detailed list of practical tips they learned with others who wish to collaborate. Even though it is not specifically meant for graduate students, we see how such a list could be of value to graduate students in particular who are learning to collaborate with diverse populations. Among such tips, the authors argue that to be successful in collaborating, we must think of ourselves as a team, "use software that facilitates and is designed for collaborative work," and "be flexible and play to individual strengths" (64–66).

In truth, today, most, if not all, fields have produced their own scholarship on collaboration, from guides to narrative accounts to self-help books. For more on strategies for learning to collaborate, we recommend another source outside our field, Karen Savage and Dominic Symonds's *Economics of Collaboration in Performance: More than the Sum of the Parts*, as it affords us an interesting way of looking at collaboration in the arts through the lens of economics and could prove helpful to our discipline, especially when we use metaphors to speak of collaborative practices.

Finally, we conclude this section with the idea that not all collaboration is good collaboration. As we have found in the scholarship previously mentioned, there are plenty of challenges that arise when people work together: the division of labor can be unequal; the task of merging multiple voices into one is always difficult; the work of some can go unnoticed. Yet while in the midst of these challenges we might discover our weaknesses, we can also find out what our unique strengths are as individuals and as team members willing to contribute in meaningful ways. Our hope is that by understanding how the disciplinary value of collaboration is lived out in material reality by scholars in the field currently, you and other graduate students might become more familiar with common obstacles, as well as best practices for collaborating in composition and rhetoric and academic work in general. It is worth further exploring the scholarship shared here on your own.

HERE'S HOW WE . . . *CAN FOSTER* *COLLABORATIVE EXPERIENCES*

We don't want to contend in this chapter that collaborative experiences should be forced upon participants. While we often ask students in our classrooms to participate in collaborative activities and assignments, we know the participants must be prepared to do so in order for the collaboration to be meaningful and effective for students. So, we first suggest here that graduate students work with their respective programs to (1) develop ways to help themselves recognize what collaboration might entail and what strategies are best for approaching such collaboration, and (2) develop actual opportunities for collaboration, whether in a classroom or elsewhere. We believe collaboration should happen elsewhere in addition to in a classroom.

To foster collaborative experiences, graduate students can work with administrators, faculty, and staff within their programs to develop the necessary curriculum, program outcomes, initiatives, and workshops necessary for developing effective collaboration. It should be a collaborative effort, that is, to build a PhD program that helps graduate students seek out meaningful opportunities for collaboration.

HERE ARE QUESTIONS TO CONSIDER . . . *WHEN ENTERING INTO COLLABORATIVE EXPERIENCES*

Once you identify an opportunity for collaboration, making sure it is the right collaborative experience for you is important. It would not be a good idea to blindly enter into an agreement to work with others without thoroughly thinking it through. To help in your decision to participate or not in a collaborative experience, we suggest you first think about what makes collaboration successful to begin with. You can do this by drawing on your previous collaborative experiences both good and bad. Then, we suggest you discuss these questions with your potential partners or at the very least keep these questions in mind before you agree to participate:

- Whom will I collaborate with, and can I work with these people? Do I have the time to make this collaborative experience successful? Am I in a position to be accountable and responsible for participating in this experience? Do our approaches to this subject complement one another effectively? Are there any conflicts of interest (ethically or legally)?

- Who isn't represented in this collaboration? Are there voices that are absent that should be present when doing work around this subject?
- What do I have to offer this group of people and this project, initiative, and/or experience? What are my strengths? Where would I like to gain experience so I can see improvement? What are my fellow collaborators' strengths, goals, and desired areas of improvement?
- What will I gain by participating in this collaborative experience? Intellectually? Professionally? Collegially? Personally?
- Do I have access to resources that will make this collaborative experience successful? If not, who might know or have access, and would it be effective to invite them to the table?

In addition to the questions above, in determining whether or not you are ready to collaborate with others, we suggest learning more about the act of collaboration by speaking with others, such as faculty and other graduate students, about their experiences with collaboration. Most likely, you will find that your faculty in your graduate program participate in all kinds of collaboration.

Last, most institutions offer access to personality inventories through their offices of career development. Explore the resources available to you and take an inventory that helps you become more aware of your tendencies and learned practices. Then answer the following reflection questions based on the Myers Briggs Personality Inventory:

1. How do you receive and direct energy? How might knowing this about yourself and your team members help you collaborate more effectively?

   - Extroverts tend to (1) receive energy from their external environment; (2) process thoughts externally through talking and discussing; (3) feel comfortable in social settings; and (4) prefer to learn by simulation or direct experience.
   - Introverts tend to (1) receive energy from their own inner world; (2) process thoughts internally through reflecting and writing; (3) feel comfortable in quiet, private spaces; and (4) prefer to learn by thinking carefully then acting.

2. How do you take in information? How might knowing this about yourself and your team members help you collaborate more effectively?

   - Sensers use the concrete information received via the five senses to focus on more objective, present realities to organize information linearly and in practical ways.
   - Intuitives use our sixth sense more, our intuition to explore patterns and imagine creative possibilities and meaning.

3. How do you make decisions? How might knowing this about yourself and your team members help you collaborate more effectively?

   - Thinkers rely on logical, analytical, cause-and-effect, or pro/con reasoning to decide.
   - Feelers lean on their values more, accessing empathy and exploring solutions that take more subjective data into account.

4. How do you organize your world? How might knowing this about yourself and your team members help you collaborate more effectively?

   - Judgers prefer the order that comes from organization, efficiency, and a well-structured schedule to help the move through their world and make decisions confidently. (Note: being a judger does not equate to being judgmental; this language is distinct in the inventory language of the Myers Briggs).
   - Perceivers prefer the opportunities afforded them through flexible scheduling and a roll-with-the-punches attitude that keep possibilities open and allows for adaptation.

HERE ARE MOVES YOU CAN MAKE TO . . .
COLLABORATE TO MAKE A DIFFERENCE

To gain experience in collaborating with others, we suggest the following activity:

Work with a group of stakeholders (such as your fellow classmates, other students in your program, alumni, and faculty) to propose a change to one of the following elements at your institution that are currently offered and are intended to prepare you for the professoriate: courses, workshops, initiatives, policies, requirements, curricula, or events. Such an activity has two primary goals: (1) to give you the opportunity to work with other stakeholders to discuss and make real changes to your current situation and (2) to help you see how stakeholders come together and collaborate on such changes. In this process, we see a secondary goal resulting from such work: to help you communicate for real audiences in ways indicative to the professoriate. In other words, this activity is another way you get practice in the profession.

Once you agree to collaborate, you must make sure you are responsible and professional in the ways you proceed to work with others in your group. This should include having open discussions with members when concerns arise, being patient and considerate of others' opinions, and having a willingness to see your work as not necessarily owned by you but owned by the group. In teaching our undergraduate courses, many of us have utilized a team agreement or similar text to help groups establish expectations, purpose, and mechanisms. We feel its prompt guides any team—not just undergraduate writers—in anticipating areas of concern and aligning in accountability early on in the project. In *Writer/Designer*, Kristin Arola, Jennifer Sheppard, and Cheryl Ball encourage collaborative groups to compose a Team Collaboration Contract to develop this sense of shared ownership and create ways to resolve conflict when it arises. Their prompt asks students to consider specifics of communication, meeting spaces, tasks, deadlines, and action steps regarding accountability in the event of a breakdown in communication or emergence of conflict (86).

MOVING FORWARD
Faculty and Graduate Program Support

HERE'S A STORY ABOUT . . . *THE FUTURE*

At NSU, our graduate program in Composition, Rhetoric, and Digital Media is a rather tight-knit community. We often get together outside our classrooms for events, workshops, and activities. As we have in the past, as graduate program faculty we will soon gather once again with our program's graduate students and alumni for another game night, a fun evening of games and conversation. During such an event, alumni will chat about what they are doing—looking for jobs, enjoying the work they are doing, trying to place articles, and so forth—while the current students will listen and ask questions. *How did you get a job? How did you write that article? What conferences should I attend?* As the evening progresses, the students will ask the alumni and faculty for more advice, and various discussions about the soon-due midterms will occur. Sprinkled throughout the event will be moments of professionalization, moments in which the future of the profession will play out in front of us—all under the ruse of a game night.

Late in the evening, the three of us will have a moment to ourselves to reflect on what has transpired. We will reminisce about our time as graduate students years earlier and how we have built on those experiences, how they have helped provide the experiences such as the one we are participating in now. We will think about our field, about our colleagues currently teaching in other graduate programs, and we will hope their departments foster the level of community and collegiality we have, that graduate students throughout the field will develop the kinds of mentoring relationships with faculty and graduate students we have experienced (both as faculty and as graduate

https://doi.org/10.7330/9781646421640.c007

students ourselves). That those students will continue on in our field and be faculty too one day. That one day they will be able to create community for their graduate students that takes into account their students' needs and helps prepare them for the future.

When the event comes to a close, when the faculty, graduate students, and alumni tire from their Mario Party and Scrabble wins and losses, we will say our goodbyes and we will start planning to gather again. The future looks promising.

HERE'S OUR ADVICE ABOUT . . . *TEACHING A DISCIPLINE VERSUS DEVELOPING A PROFESSIONAL*

As our time researching together has neared its conclusion, we have reflected more and more on the importance of using this book to help current and future graduate students. We believe moving forward, that is, working to improve what we do to prepare graduate students for the professoriate, will need to be a team effort, one that is collaborative and that involves all stakeholders: graduate students, faculty, administrators, and staff.

Throughout this book, we share many calls for action—from our own work and from others'. As we look to the future, we must intentionally build on these calls, not ignore them. As we have shown, there have been several unanswered calls in scholarship in the past decades: provide graduate students with a range of career options that more accurately represents the job market; give students a behind-the-scenes look at what life is really like as an assistant professor; demystify the operations of higher education, and so forth. We must do a better job identifying what these calls require in terms of resources—financial and otherwise—and how we can work together to take them on. We must conduct rigorous programmatic assessments, as well as more thorough quantitative and qualitative studies on graduate students and new faculty, in order to determine whether we are successful in our endeavors.

Experiential learning, specifically professional development, should be integrated into the very curriculum of graduate programs. Besides the list of things our participants indicated they wished they had learned in graduate school, we compiled an additional list of ways graduate schools could better to prepare students for life in the professoriate. The following list is not an all-inclusive list, however, as creating such a list would be nearly impossible given the unique situations at every institution. Yet, we feel such a list could provide a more comprehensive starting point for revisions of graduate program curriculum. We believe graduate students and new faculty should learn how to

- work with an HR department;
- network and collaborate with colleagues in other departments;
- participate in and/or lead a committee, such as a curriculum committee;
- build rapport with department chairs, deans, provosts, and presidents of their institutions;
- contribute to a faculty senate;
- serve as a student advisor or mentor;
- market themselves and their departments, classes, and programs to institution insiders and outsiders.

Miller et al. suggest, and we agree, that we must do more to make "the profession *as a subject* a part of the curriculum"—not just the discipline (404). One way to do so is to help graduate students learn what being a new faculty member is actually like by participating in authentic experiences in which they meet, interview, and shadow new faculty.

Moreover, graduate students should study new faculty at a variety of institutions to be able to consider all possibilities for their career paths. Miller et al. write that programs could be more accountable if they and their students developed more of an awareness of the vast career options for graduates, not just at colleges and universities but beyond academia (402). We agree. We must develop such awareness. Yet, how do we do so? How can we reflect on the veracity of our graduate programs in sincere ways to ensure another study like ours or Miller et al.'s doesn't echo these same findings in another twenty years?

To begin with, we must provide students with more options for career paths, and we must let them try these out, giving them authentic learning experiences. In other words, we must do more than just talk about the options. We must let students participate in them.

Doctoral programs would do well, too, to focus more on problem solving, providing a variety of real-life situations new faculty encounter rather than just generalizing the faculty experience. For instance, graduate programs could develop relationships with a variety of sister institutions where students can see other writing faculty at work, including faculty at work at two-year colleges. As has been discussed, many of our participants pointed out that their doctoral programs focused too heavily on preparing students to take on research positions at R1 institutions, ignoring a plethora of other options graduate students could explore. Many of the participants wished they had been given the chance to see more possibilities for their degree.

The future will require that graduate students (yourself included) actively participate in helping shape their doctoral programs—from sitting on committees to writing narratives of their experiences to creating curriculum—so as to best provide current and future graduate students with authentic, meaningful experiences that translate into the professoriate. A first step, one we believe is vitally important and one you can take now, is to work together with the stakeholders in your program and institution to create experiential learning opportunities.

HERE'S WHAT OUR RESEARCH SAYS ABOUT . . .
THE DANGER OF A SINGLE STORY

As researchers, we know we must be critical of our work and the advice we give. Our study is but one study, and we recognize its shortcomings. We know that, in terms of sharing our own stories as collaborators and researchers, our story of this study is context specific, that what we say about our experiences researching might not be true of all researchers who collaborate on a study. It is not the only story, and we have worked diligently throughout this work to share the narratives of our research participants along with the more generalizable findings from our survey.

Our field values research that embraces feminist research methodology, which is a set of ethical philosophies and corresponding research practices that require researchers to be aware of their stances, power positions, and responsibility to represent others in scholarship. Throughout our time working together, there were plenty of moments we stepped away from our study and our data to participate in reflections and discussions about our own positions as faculty members. To mimic these times when we stepped away, we have included stories throughout this book that invite readers to learn more about how our research came to be. As we have found, research is not a streamlined, highly organized, and linear endeavor and neither is writing a book about research. To this end, we felt compelled to provide stories about what happened in the past several years as our research unfolded. Many of these stories are about us working through the research process. In our study, for example, we were acutely aware of our role in the phenomena we were observing. At one point in our lives, we too experienced them. In their chapter "The Construction of Research Problems and Methods," Pamela Takayoshi, Elizabeth Tomlinson, and Jennifer Castillo write that "an (ongoing, continual) examination of our assumptions as researchers, as scholars, and as people enacting relationships through our research practices is important for understanding the potentials and limits of our research" (99). Furthermore, as they contend, "ignoring how subjectivity shapes our research keeps us from being able to account for it as an influence" (112). Throughout our process, we felt a need to account for these concerns, as well as to reflectively consider the impact of our subjectivity, both as a team and as individuals. To help us maintain awareness both in our research process and in our conversations, we even recorded our meetings. In fact, the voice recordings of our meetings provided us with not only an account of our processes as researchers but also with an immediate and constant reminder that we, too, are a part of the community.

We also know the data we collected cannot reflect all new faculty in our field but rather that it only reflects the nearly two hundred new assistant professors in our study. Our study, for example, didn't include those who took on positions as part-timers or as adjuncts. Those populations are an important part of our field. We concentrated on assistant professors given the resources we had at our disposal and the time we had to conduct our study. In other words, to make this a manageable project, we had to focus on one population. Also, there are certainly other positions inside and outside academia that someone might obtain once they graduate from a doctoral program in our field, and those are worth studying too.

We also recognize that our population did not have many men or people of color, and that different populations of people face different challenges. The fact that white women more than any other demographic made up our population was not a methodological oversight but rather a reflection of our field's makeup, which speaks to a history of inequity and exclusion that enabled a lack of diversity in our field and led to the barriers of entry that minorities in the field face. For example, as has been pointed out by many scholars in our field, people of color, especially women, are expected to do more service (VanHaitsma and Ceraso 223–224). The field has a responsibility to explore the underlying ideologies and prejudices that inform such an expectation, as well as other unique challenges that specific populations of new faculty face when their identities as professors intersect with socially constructed categories of race, class, gender, and (dis)ability. We have already imagined how other studies could fill the gaps in our study and want to encourage future studies to consider various populations.

Finally, it is necessary to acknowledge that, to a considerable extent, it is not possible to prepare a graduate student for every possible scenario. The more holistic disciplinary focus we learn through our programs indeed prepares us in some ways for critical thinking in academic contexts and for any combination of responsibilities in teaching, research, service, and administration (depending upon the focus of our programs and our own interests). But much of what we learn is via a one-way street: discussions with mentors, in workshops, and in seminars, all telling students what they can expect but never giving them an opportunity for firsthand experience. What are missing are the kinds of experiential learning opportunities that provide a two-way street, so to speak, for graduate students.

HERE'S WHAT SCHOLARSHIP SAYS ABOUT . . . *EXPERIENTIAL LEARNING*

Because we were limited by the technologies we used and the time we had to conduct our study, we were not able to identify and research all possibilities for experiential learning. We also recognize we were not able to ask more questions in our survey and in our interviews that could further reveal what other specific experiential learning opportunities would be beneficial to those preparing not just for positions as assistant professors but for other positions as well. We are aware of the limitations of our recommendations regarding experiential learning; however, we hope they address the majority of graduate students who seek full-time employment in academia.

Scholarship on experiential learning confirms that concrete experiences followed with active reflection lead to abstract generalizations that go on to inform future experiences and behaviors (Kolb and Kolb). For some of our readers, current experiential learning may mean working in writing centers or working as assistant WPAs during graduate school with the hope of applying what they learn to teaching in a classroom later on. While those experiences may be commonplace, opportunities for more diverse experiential learning, the kind that takes into account the various responsibilities, decisions, and negotiations faculty make, are few and far between. Any opportunity for students to learn in an authentic manner that encourages the kind of learning cycle described by Alice Kolb and David Kolb would be a strong effort toward preparing graduate students for work as a faculty member.

Programmatic assessment is no doubt required by our graduate institutions and is conducted frequently. As you work with your program's stakeholders and look collectively across program learning outcomes, consider whether any of those outcomes—or methods of achieving them—are informed by the National Society for Experiential Education's "Eight Principles of Experiential Learning": intention, preparedness and planning, authenticity, reflection, orientation and training, monitoring and continuous improvement, assessment and evaluation, and acknowledgment. In addition, consider these principles in the context of our field and in shaping programmatic design and delivery for the future:

- **Intention**: When we think of intention, we should think about the purposes of a program and its objectives and how those include or exclude students' purposes and objectives for being in graduate school. For example, if we don't intentionally build our programs to include preparation for a variety of academic careers and positions, it's not just going to happen organically; students will see only one model of institution—the one at which they receive their doctorate. What values and assumptions inform the intentions of your doctoral program? And how does your program's intentions for you align with your own intentions for the future?

- **Preparedness and Planning**: There will always be an element of foundational professional development in doctoral study, but the balance between preparation, planning, and, we would add, experience should be specifically considered. To what extent does your program encourage you to plan ahead? To prepare to "leave the nest" long before degree conferral? To experience all facets of the field?

- **Authenticity**: One of the goals of this book is to help students participate in authentic experiences. Our interviewees, for instance, spoke about being protected from politics in graduate school. We think this approach might be misguided since we believe exposing students to the realities of academic employment is important for their future success. Where can you seek opportunities to get your feet wet, so to speak, to roll up your sleeves and have different authentic academic experiences?

- **Reflection**: Active, critical reflection is essential for any learning experience and for graduate students to be able to understand the past, revise the present, and inform the

future. How often do you reflect on your experiences and
how those experiences are shaped by you, your program,
the field, and your institution? How does your program
encourage reflection and where might other opportunities
for reflection be present?

- **Orientation and Training**: Consider how collaborations and
  partnerships could help you prepare for authentic learning. What are some ways your program can make moves to
  orient you to the field and train you for all aspects of it in
  real ways? For example, bringing a guest speaker typically
  involves an (albeit brief) orientation for the guest to the
  graduate program and its students. What if we gave more
  time to this? What if we sincerely considered our program's
  gaps and oriented our guests or community members to
  help address them? What if, in turn, the guests help orient
  and train our students to future possible realities in the
  professoriate?

- **Monitoring and Continuous Improvement**: Any course
  includes a series of formative and summative assessments.
  Formative assessments provide benchmarks along the way,
  as well as feedback loops to allow for growth. Summative
  assessments measure performance of learning outcomes
  at conclusive or pivotal moments during the course. How
  do we structure our programs to allow for monitoring and
  continuous improvement? Who helps our students gain a
  bird's-eye view of their development as professionals? Who
  helps them set benchmarks?

- **Assessment and Evaluation**: Graduate programs in composition and rhetoric assess graduate students on written
  work, mostly. They support them in learning the language,
  ideologies, and body of knowledge of our field. How do
  we support them and coach them through professionalism
  opportunities? Is this support formal or informal? Do we
  conduct sincere annual evaluations intended for the growth
  of the student? How do we know we are successful in preparing our graduate students for the future? The Higher
  Educational Research Institute conducts exit surveys of
  all graduate students. But how do individual programs
  check in with students in their first three years of full-time
  employment? Do we assume advisors and mentors carry this
  torch? Do we value that work anywhere on our CVs?

- **Acknowledgment**: Long-term goals must be made up of
  short-term gains in order for anyone to sustain motivation,

interest, and growth. Outside of the context of coursework, for which students receive a grade, how are students
acknowledged for their efforts in doctoral study? How
are students celebrated as they reach programmatic mile-
stones? How are faculty and mentors acknowledged for
the invisible labor that is mentoring, advising, and alumni
networking?

In addition to learning more about experiential learning
and how we can include it more robustly in our programs, we
can turn to recent scholarship that can help us explore different ways to better prepare graduate students. In a 2017 special
issue of *Teaching English in the Two-Year College*, for instance, the
Two-Year College Association (TYCA) put forth its guidelines
for preparing future faculty to teach at two-year colleges. The
guidelines make clear how graduate programs could specifically
integrate ways students could gain experience and expertise in
teaching at a two-year college, including the chance to develop
curricula for two-year colleges and to collaborate with area two-
year colleges near their universities (Calhoon-Dillahunt et al.
9). These experiences working with sister institutions, developing curricula, and so forth are the experiences that will help students when they imagine the possibilities of their future.

HERE'S HOW WE . . . *CHANGE IN THREE SPECIFIC WAYS*

With these calls for action and this scholarship in mind, our
final chapter is about looking forward and offering three specific suggestions for ways we might use our findings to begin
improving support at the institutional and disciplinary levels.
Our field has done quite a lot to help graduate students, and
thus new faculty, as we explain in this book. Yet, given the changing nature of our positions at a variety of institutions coupled
with the budget cuts many of these institutions are facing, we
wondered if the field could do more. Our answer is yes.

There are certainly opportunities to do more at the conferences we attend and to do more with the position statements
our field's organizations put forth, but we see this *more* being

implemented on even deeper levels, in how we teach graduate students, how we write about what we do in our field, and how we share our stories and our discipline with those outside our field. We believe, as does Keith Hjortshoj, that "because *being* a good graduate student is a process of *becoming* something else—a good scholar—individuals are most likely to succeed in program environments and advising systems that acknowledge the difficulties of this transition and provide the most support through the process. Varying levels and qualities of support largely account for differences in completion rates of more than 30 percent among PhD programs in the same fields at different institutions" (Denecke 2005, 7). We recognize there are more suggestions than just the three we offer in this chapter. However, we see these as a good starting place from which we can all—you, your professors, your (future) colleagues—have conversations about how to move forward as a field and the ways we can highlight our successes so far and improve on the areas where we have identified gaps.

Foremost, we need stronger resources for graduate students and new faculty, such as profession-specific scholarship, financial support, access to materials, and a balance of personal and professional time. Second, we need continued (and evolving) professional development at hiring institutions that includes teaching faculty to be mentors. This development should be informed by the discipline and by you, as well as the institutional cultures you will be joining. And finally, both our field and hiring institutions need a better awareness of the roles you will take on as new faculty members, specifically regarding day-to-day experiences.

1. Develop Even More Support Resources

In addition to looking more closely at what new faculty wished they had learned prior to becoming a faculty member, we want to cast a wider net here and look at what does exist already (that is, the resources new faculty have access to) and speak about ways our field as a whole could improve upon them. There are, for instance, quite a few resources that help new faculty, and that is reassuring. But it would be in our best interest to be critical of these to ensure that what they have to offer does in fact prepare and support new faculty. For example, while we need more studies on graduate programs, we also need more studies on new faculty and specific ways we can learn from each of these types of studies.

Search *Amazon* for books about being a new college faculty member and you will find hundreds, from guides to handbooks. They all claim to be full of advice, from navigating institutional politics to lecturing in a classroom. However, while such resources outline the expectations new faculty might encounter in any field, the advice is often too broad and irrelevant to be of any substantial value to our field in particular. Pamela VanHaitsma and Steph Ceraso write in their guide on horizontal mentoring for new faculty:

> Published guidance is necessarily generalized and, when graduate students and new faculty encounter it in relative isolation, information that was meant to be helpful may simply exacerbate anxieties. Once we have become familiar with the general guidance, the real challenge becomes finding ways to adapt that advice in order to apply it within very specific rhetorical situations. These situations vary based on not only our own positioning, as Grollman details, but also the specificities of our institutions, departments, programs, colleagues, and students. (211)

Therefore, we want to caution you that the resources, in terms of scholarship, listed in our Works Cited and in the reading list below, should only be used as a starting point for conducting your own research into what you need to do to prepare for the professoriate. Likewise, while there are plenty of books outside our field on (1) what it means to be a professor and (2) the many responsibilities professors take on, such as mentoring, we believe we shouldn't have to look outside our field for help. Our field is diverse in the sense that faculty may take on a wide variety of positions housed in a variety of departments, centers, and institutions. We must be able to see the unique situations those in our field find themselves in as new faculty.

Table 7.1. Reading List

---

1. *First Semester: Graduate Students, Teaching Writing, and the Challenge of Middle Ground* by Jessica Restaino (2012)

2. "Resistance and Identity Formation: The Journey of the Graduate Student-Teacher" by Jennifer Grouling (2015)

3. *Stories of Mentoring* by Michelle F. Eble and Lynée Lewis Gaillet (2008)

4. "Graduate Teaching Assistants' Development of Expertise in Teaching First-Year Composition" by Carolyn Anne Wisniewski (2014)

5. "Collaborative Development: Reflective Mentoring for GTAs" by Jule Wallis and Adrienne Jankens (2017)

6. "GTA Preparation as a Model for Cross-Tier Collaboration at North Carolina State University: A Program Profile" by Casie Fedukovich and Megan Hall (2016)

7. *From Student to Scholar: A Guide to Writing Through the Dissertation Stage* by Keith Hjortshoj (2019)

8. *Supporting Graduate Student Writers: Research, Curriculum, & Program Design* edited by Steve Simpson, Nigel A. Caplan, Michelle Cox, and Talinn Phillips (2016)

9. *The Academic Job Search Handbook*, 5th ed., by Julia Miller Vick, Jennifer S. Furlong, and Rosanne Lurie (2016)

10. *The Working Lives of New Writing Center Directors* by Nicole I. Caswell, Jackie Grutsch McKinney, and Rebecca Jackson (2016)

11. *A Faculty Guide for Succeeding in the Academe* by Darla J. Twale (2013)

Resources, in general, do us no good if we do not learn from them in productive ways or if they simply further grand narratives. So, we ask that you find ways to use any scholarship cautiously and critically, to question it in relationship to your own realities and those of others. Indeed, we need to be able to capture what life is like in our field as new faculty and learn from it. But, time and again, studies about graduate programs or new faculty make the same calls for improvement, calls that, in many ways, go unanswered. As we discuss earlier, for instance, Miller et al.'s study called for graduate programs to show graduate students career options other than researching at an R1 institution. Yet, in our study over twenty years later, we found new faculty are still wishing their graduate programs had shown them career options other than researching at an R1 institution.

What we are suggesting here is the need to do something with this scholarship that involves more than just reading it. In what ways, we wonder, can these calls have a bigger impact not just on you, not just on new faculty, but on all faculty and those who do and do not support faculty effectively? It seems to us that sometimes when scholarship is published, especially as narrative, people read it, nod their heads in agreement knowing they had a similar experience, but then leave it at that. Then, another narrative comes along, people read it, nod their heads again, and leave it at that. How can we, as a field, take advantage of this type of scholarship to effect real changes?

Moreover, to help prepare you to become new faculty, you should encourage your program to more explicitly incorporate field-specific resources such as the WPA council's, NCTE's, and CCCC's position statements and teach you how to use these to effectively advocate for the various kinds of work you will undoubtedly do. The participants in our study belonged to a wide range of professional organizations including CCCC (the highest membership among participants at 73.4%), NCTE (the second-highest membership among participants at 63.7%), RSA (42.3%), and WPA (35.2%). A smaller percent were members of MLA, ATTW, TYCA, IWCA, PCA/ACA, FemRhet, and ABC.

The CCCC's "Statement of Professional Guidance for New Faculty Members" (Conference) can help prepare graduates on the job market to ask effective and useful questions of their interviewing institutions and departments. CCCC's "Scholarship in Rhetoric, Writing, and Communication: Guidelines for Faculty, Deans, and Chairs" (Conference) and the WPA's "Evaluating the Intellectual Work of Writing Program Administration" (Council) can be useful resources for new faculty to provide to hiring departments not expressly familiar with our field or not chaired by members of it. Similarly, specialized statements on work with technology or TESOL can have immeasurable benefits for new faculty struggling to categorize their work in ways institutionally recognizable for contract renewal, tenure, promotion, and so forth. A crucial element that seems lacking in our graduate and new-faculty professional development seems to be demonstrating how these kinds of resources can be used as tools for self-advocacy.

Additionally, institutional-based studies exploring new-faculty needs, habits, and experiences can provide a more robust understanding of how to prepare graduate students and new faculty to cultivate dynamic professional identities. Using narratives of junior faculty who were tasked with teaching and developing undergraduate degrees in writing, Giberson et al. found that new faculty "need a working knowledge of the machinery of academic production; of the specific institutional, political, and historical contexts where they will labor; of the bureaucratic, imaginative, and rhetorical work of program development, and of the possible consequences—positive and negative—of this work." Following Giberson et al.'s lead, we posit that, for institutional studies to be most useful, they will need to be visible and relatively accessible, even to those outside the specific institution's local community.

As a field, it is imperative that we know the needs of our newest professional colleagues, not only for the purposes of better preparing our graduate students for faculty positions in the discipline but also because a candidate for any position should have a confident understanding of the job's expectations. Our study demonstrates that many new faculty vaguely perceive expectations and receive little communication that might help clarify those expectations. In the same way we survey employers for undergraduate career-development purposes, we should—at the very least—develop a generalized understanding of professional expectations for faculty in academia. One key skill our participants identified needing in their new positions was resource discovery (e.g., funding and its parameters, teaching and learning professional development, etc.).

Resource support doesn't have to come just in the form of books or guides or professional statements. It can also take on other forms, such as financial support, material support, or time support. The opening story of this book sheds light on the challenges faculty face when trying to perform their duties. One such challenge is securing the necessary funding to (1) conduct research, (2) purchase classroom supplies and equipment, and (3) engage in service. On our survey, we asked new faculty participants whether they had received paid course release, travel funding, or internal grants. Nearly 75% of our participants said they received paid course release, 88% said they received travel funding, and nearly 50% said they received internal grants. However, while in their graduate programs, 39% of participants indicated they received paid course release (30% said it was not available), 91% of participants received travel funding, and 57.4% of participants received internal grants. Furthermore, looking closely at the CVs we collected, we saw that our interviewees listed a variety of kinds of financial support they earned as graduate students and as new faculty, from internal and external grants to fellowships and awards. We feel encouraged by these numbers, as they speak to the support both faculty and graduates receive currently. But we do recognize that to earn this support, students and faculty had to work hard, write numerous documents, research, plan, negotiate, and so forth, all of which takes time. We also know as budgets shrink, these numbers may shrink too. Therefore, both the field and our institutions must be proactive in providing financial support to graduate students and new faculty and teaching them how to seek it, negotiate for it, and use it effectively.

For example, our field can find more creative ways to financially support graduate students and new faculty at institutions where funding is limited. To do so, we must find ways to teach the processes for writing grants and provide grant-writing mentors who can help with those processes, including helping graduate students and new faculty locate funding opportunities and analyze examples of previous successful grant attempts. However, we also must recognize that grants can't be the only source of funding. While we do have grants in the humanities we could rely on, (CCCC, after all, funded part of this research project), they are limited in number and in award amount. Therefore, we must to be able to support research projects and other activities, big and small, such as helping graduate students and new faculty attend more conferences. To do so, we must pressure our organizations into helping us find ways we can raise funding at the same time we lower costs for such things.

2. Formalize Professional Development

Links between our field and studies of faculty development are noticeable, particularly after what many have called the "turn toward pedagogy" in our field in the 1990s and early 2000s (Stenberg, 2–3). In fact, scholars over the years, such as Iris Artze-Vega et al., have identified many similarities. In their study, Artze-Vega et al. draw on Peter Felten, Alan Kalish, Allison Pingree, and Kathryn Plank to define faculty development as "a profession dedicated to helping colleges and universities function effectively as teaching and learning communities" (164). Artze-Vega et al. argue that "comp/rhet scholars and practitioners typically experience deliberate training and develop insights into teaching that are relevant across disciplines" (166–167). In other words, they contend that because of our training and because of the nature of our field and its affinity for teaching, faculty in our field are better positioned to take on roles as faculty developers who work with faculty in all disciplines. Indeed, our field is poised to do a lot that others cannot and do not do, such as participate in assessments, develop student resources, train others in student-related activities, and so on, expertise that expands beyond our discipline. We also have experience in writing across and in the disciplines that we can draw from, for instance, in order to work with other disciplines to provide the professional development faculty need.

Truly, faculty development is where we could potentially do the most to help new faculty transition out of their time as graduate students. Artze-Vega et al. conclude their study with faculty-development recommendations to better prepare students for life as a faculty member. For instance, they argue that "larger graduate programs could offer courses that focus primarily on faculty development, both as a potential career path and as an area of scholarly inquiry" (175). If such a course is not possible, they suggest at the very least that "existing courses could be expanded through a more explicit emphasis on faculty development as a potential component of their future careers" (175–176). Their conclusions harken back to several calls for more serious study of what and how faculty development can help new faculty in our field. This effort would not only serve our graduate students' career paths but would also prepare new faculty for seeking development opportunities, whether or not their hiring institution offers them. Our study found that new faculty must balance multimembership, so let us be explicit about that as early as we can in our graduate program studies.

In addition, Stenberg argues that as a field we must move away from teacher training and concentrate more on teacher development. She argues "for encounters with pedagogical scholarship that portray the teacher as an ongoing learner, opportunities to reflect on the relationship between pedagogies from which we've learned and the pedagogies we seek to enact, and teacher learning that is equally dependent upon community and curriculum" (134). By learning encounters that foster teacher development, she means we must "position new (and part-time) teachers as knowers" (135), each capable of contributing their own thoughts and insights into teaching.

In her book *Rhetorical Strategies for Professional Development*, Elizabeth Keller argues for professional development as rhetorical acts. We extend her claims in the context of our study; professional development is not just about growth and improvement in regard to one's job responsibilities. It should and can be rhetorical acts that aid in one's development as a professional through the experimentation and evaluation of possible selves.

As our interviews reveal, Tahir's institution has invested in professional support for faculty. However, that is not the case at every institution. Thankfully, though, when graduate students and new faculty are ill supported at their institutions, organizations within our field work to support them, whether through informal or formal programs and events. Events like the Mentoring@Cs Breakfast and the Research Network Forum at the Conference on College Composition and Communication's annual convention, for instance, enable newcomers to work with experienced faculty. Most recently, the Council of Writing Program Administrators' graduate organization (WPAGO) began facilitating a mentoring program at CCCC, intentionally pairing graduate students with faculty in positions the students would like to have when they graduate. We are encouraged by these and hope in the future we will see more.

Organizations outside our field (even ones not tied to a particular discipline) can help as well. For example, the Professional and Organizational Development Network, in its "Strategic Plan," provides "professional development and a community of practice for scholars and practitioners of educational development, and . . . serve[s] as a leading voice on matters related to teaching and learning in higher education." The National Center for Faculty Development & Diversity (NCFDD) offers coaching on "four key areas that help you achieve extraordinary writing and research productivity while maintaining a full and healthy life off campus." Organizations such as these offer more opportunities to experience and network with a variety of faculty.

However, while these organizations are helpful in many ways, we argue our field can do more. After your graduate program, you will continue to need support when you become a full-time faculty member that extends beyond what our field and what a before-the-first-semester-begins orientation can currently provide. Places like professional- or faculty-development centers (sometimes referred to as *teaching and learning centers*) on campuses—if you are lucky enough to have one—can provide one avenue of continuous support hiring institutions can invest in and the discipline can help shape. In fact, Tahir talked at length about how valuable such a place was for her in learning to navigate institutional politics as a new faculty member.

If a center is not feasible, you may need to work with your hiring institution to find other ways to secure faculty-development support. As a result of their study, Miller et al., for instance, suggest designating someone in the department to "serve as something like a 'professional development resource coordinator'" who would be in charge of "running professional development workshops throughout the year" (403). In serving in this position, faculty would have a front-row view of the challenges new faculty like yourself face. So, such a person would not only be a good resource for new faculty in providing professional development but could also be instrumental in researching new faculty and making changes to programs based on such research.

Keller's model of Investment Mentoring is yet another approach we could take to provide professional-development opportunities (*Rhetorical Strategies*). We believe, as does Keller, that professional development in academia doesn't mean indoctrination. Rather, it is a kind of investment that allows for autonomy and agency on the part of the new faculty member. There is an important distinction between enculturation and rhetorical professional-development strategies that empower individuals to prioritize their values before the values of the institution. Often, models of mentoring or professional-development inherently imply that the values of the institution reign supreme, while an approach like Keller's is a more symbiotic negotiation of priorities that account for your values as a teacher, scholar, citizen, leader, and individual. This is a fine line—and one hard to perceive as a graduate student who is being "disciplined," given that graduate students don't often have the full experience of being a faculty member.

This avenue of professional development should include more opportunities for the right kinds of mentoring and the teaching of mentoring. If we compare our survey results with Miller et al.'s survey on graduate students in composition and rhetoric programs, we see some similarities that indicate to us that over the past twenty years, programs in our field have continued to succeed in several ways, especially in the quality of their faculty and their ability to be good mentors. In Miller et al.'s survey, graduates were presented with a list of program features and experiences and asked to rate their satisfaction. As the report states,

> On the whole, graduate students clearly seemed impressed with some central components of their programs, especially the quality of their faculty mentors and daily interactions with them. Over

90% of respondents expressed satisfaction with the competence
of their mentors and with the individualized assistance they
provide; and a full 65% claimed the higher, "extremely satisfied"
level regarding faculty quality and competence. (395)

At the beginning of our study, we asked participants about
the faculty in their graduate programs and their work with
them. We wanted to know what kinds of relationships they
had with their instructors when they were graduate students.
For example, 44.7% *agreed somewhat* and 42.5% *strongly agreed*
their faculty were effective teachers, while 37% *agreed somewhat*
and 46.9% *strongly agreed* their faculty were effective mentors.
Participants talked not only about their mentors as having a
positive impact on their lives but also about how they sought
mentors with whom they could specifically identify and wanted
to emulate once they graduated. In particular, participants Sam
and Lee talked about the importance of being able to work with
a mentor who had the same professional interests. Lee expli-
cated that her mentor was someone she identified with really
strongly. She told us that while there were other faculty members involved with her doctoral program and that she would
most likely have found a professional identity, Lee didn't believe
it would have been quite as easy if she hadn't had a faculty member who she felt embodied the sort of professional identity she
wanted to embody herself.

Based on these findings, we argue that as a discipline, we
have some work to do in order to ensure our faculty in our graduate programs are not only effective teachers but also effective
mentors. We must find ways we can both teach in effective ways
and provide support via mentoring students. One way is to pair
graduate students with nongraduate program faculty, perhaps
those who solely teach first-year composition courses, giving students an opportunity to learn from a colleague in their field but
outside their doctoral program.

Moreover, in our study, we asked participants about how
their graduate program faculty prepared them for the teaching, research, service, and administrative work they do now.
Participants felt faculty most adequately taught students to

conduct research effectively and least adequately taught students to engage in service effectively. This finding was common throughout our study. That is, we can see graduate students will be hired to do more than just research but that research was prioritized almost inequitably by their graduate programs. So, from this finding, we gather that graduate programs are doing well to prepare students to conduct research but that they could do more to provide opportunities to students, particularly when it comes to service. To do so, programs might begin by thinking carefully about how they mentor students and how that mentorship will help students be well-rounded individuals who have experience in teaching, research, service, and administrative work from a professional perspective.

Developing good mentoring systems is paramount to helping graduate students succeed both in their doctoral programs and in the professoriate. Such systems must be multifaceted as a result. In terms of graduate programs, as our study finds, our field is doing a good job providing students with good mentors though, as in all things, there are areas in which we could improve. For example, Miller et al. suggest that "a good mentoring program should involve specific kinds of 'shadowing' activity" in that students should do more than just "observe their mentors as teachers for a term, watching, discussing, and asking questions as those teachers plan courses, prepare classroom activities, and actually teach;" that is, they should be able to see their mentors doing all their "daily business" (405). In terms of mentoring new faculty, we don't see a reason such mentoring should cease once students graduate and go on to the professoriate. We believe new faculty should be able to shadow other faculty and see what it is like to be a faculty member at their institution. But, mentors must be taught how to mentor, and learning to mentor should be something we teach in graduate programs.

Miller et al.'s study came out in the late 1990s when composition and rhetoric graduate programs were growing. Yet, calls for better mentoring within such programs, as well as in mentoring new faculty, haven't ceased. Since the 90s, our field has reiterated time and again the need to look more deeply at what we mean by mentoring. Take E. Shelley Reid's 2008 call, arguing that good teachers don't necessarily make good mentors and that mentoring doesn't necessarily come naturally to all, that in some crucial ways, it must be taught (51). She writes that "to create a successful mentoring program for new composition teachers, mentors and WPAs need to acknowledge that peer mentoring is an institutional endeavor, and treat it as such. To provide guidance to all participants, they must design mentoring protocols and describe clear boundaries to guide all participants" (53). We couldn't agree more, and we encourage our readers to seek out mentoring opportunities from a diverse group of people.

In fact, there are many types of mentors: there are senior faculty mentors for new faculty in and out of a department, which means mentors could be in the discipline or not; there are administrator mentors who are charged with mentoring several new faculty at once; there are new faculty who mentor new faculty. Each of these scenarios comes with challenges, however. Effective mentoring practices have the power to shape institutional, departmental, and field-specific values, practices, and pedagogies in addition to the identity of a member of those communities. They do not—and should not be assumed to—simply emerge organically when a department member is assigned to a new hire. As Reid notes, for instance, "Mentor-relationships can be compromised when the mentor who is supposed to provide support and counsel—and to whom a mentee should be able to admit confusion or failure—is also a person who provides formal job-evaluations of the mentee" (59). This is especially precarious for a new faculty member who may not yet know the dynamics of the institutional culture. Reid outlines four necessities for good mentoring: "[1] self-knowledge and goal-setting exercises; [2] content knowledge about educating adult teachers; [3] strategy information about interacting with mentees; and [4] conceptual approaches to encourage mentors' reflection and integration of new ideas and practices" (62). Preparation may mean graduate students and new faculty who will be mentors should (1) attend workshops where they are given the opportunity to learn and reflect on how to be a good mentor and (2) shadow mentors to see firsthand what good mentoring looks like. This kind of experiential learning is crucial to seeing the rhetorical strategies successful mentoring requires.

In her exploration of the Investment Model of mentoring, Keller challenges the blurring of lines between enculturation and an individual's professional development, advocating a model that "makes space for the self-identification of an individual" (30). She maintains that successful mentoring is the result of deliberate, systemic rhetorical strategies. As members of a field, an institution, a department, and a graduate program, we believe it is critical that we consider these Investment Mentoring principles proposed by Keller: (1) provide mentoring benchmarks that include acknowledgment of power differentials in the relationship and the fact that we are all learners; (2) plan and manage the mentoring process or relationship, which includes deciding on not only goals and outcomes but also on logistical details such as where and when you will meet; and (3) hold one another accountable so the relationship can be successful—including acknowledgment of achievement and assessment of the value of the relationship and discontinuing said relationship, if necessary (121–124). Her principles can serve as a framework for critically reflecting on and crafting what we do to mentor and what we do to teach mentoring.

3. Capture the Day-to-Day Life Activities of New Faculty

In her collection *Kitchen Cooks, Plate Twirlers, and Troubadors: Writing Program Administrators Tell Their Stories*, Diana George has gathered narratives of the profession through vivid images of balance—the way a chef must orchestrate the line to ensure all food is quality and delivered on time; the way a plate twirler starts small and then adds more and more plates that must be kept spinning; the way a troubadour constantly revises their singing and playing in light of audience response. The common theme among these images is simultaneity: balancing, juggling, and multitasking. Our study's participants identified balancing the tetrad as a prominent obstacle in their first three years as full-time faculty. Often, teaching, research, service, and administration are treated as distinct, independent things rather than what they are: dependent on, intertwined with, and bound by one another. Scholars in our field should treat teaching, research, service, and administration as happening at the same time because the work of a faculty member requires simultaneity—the more intentional and reflective the practice, the better. Now, it is neither recommended nor possible most days to stick to a plan or an agenda due to the dynamic nature of academic workplaces and the variety of job responsibilities we often take on. However, intention goes a long way. In this book we discuss many strategies for responding to the simultaneity of the work we do—a more accurate canvas of the variety of positions and contexts for our work; better graduate preparation in graduate study; more strategic professional development as new faculty; evidence-based mentoring practices; time-management strategies; work/life-balance approaches; and so forth—balance being perhaps the most important aspiration in managing one's time and responsibilities.

In her study of composition and rhetoric faculty, Christine Tulley identifies time as the most cited obstacle in efforts to develop effective writing habits (3). The irony of her participants being prominent figures in a field of writing studies is not lost on Tulley; we should be poised to effectively produce scholarly writing for publication. And yet, "[w]e know what circumstances hinder some rhetoric and composition faculty from writing for scholarly publication, but little about the disciplinary practices that make successful writing faculty productive" (8). Even when such knowledge is produced—as in Tulley's study—our field has the added challenge of defying traditional notions of what "counts" as scholarship in the larger contexts of our institutions and higher education. We bring this to your attention because scholarship is an inherently values-based aspect of our careers in academia. As faculty, in order to produce, practice, and serve in ways that reflect our own values first—and then respond to disciplinary and institutional values—we must know who we are and what matters most to us, holistically, as individuals.

Considering the extent to which our participants struggled to achieve work/life balance, we wonder whether our work in preparing graduate students for work in the field comes at the expense of considering our students wholly—a practice we tout in undergraduate composition pedagogy but may not always deliberately implement with junior colleagues. As graduate students, you may be so intent on looking outward, working to establish yourselves as insiders in the field, that you may neglect to look inward, reflecting to develop yourselves as an individual first and foremost. As we say in the introduction, if—and that's a big *if*—this study could be generalized into one takeaway, we would share the following with our field's newest faculty members and those like you who are studying to become them: values matter—disciplinary, institutional, and academic—but none *should* matter more than your own. As important as it is to experiment with pedagogical and critical theories of teaching, research, and academic labor, it is essential that you experiment with possible selves as you develop in our profession.

Despite the calls for improvement we make in this chapter, we acknowledge what the field is doing well. Above all, participants in our study were mostly satisfied with their graduate programs. When asked what changes they would make if they were to begin their career again, nearly 65% of participants said they would definitely or probably choose the same doctoral program, and nearly 73% said they would definitely or probably choose the same professional path. These numbers show we are doing a good job but that there is always room for improvement, especially because when we help new faculty, we help all faculty, and benefits to our field, our institutions, and—most important—our students grow exponentially. As we note in the introduction, practitioners in our field don't tend to think "good is good enough." We are achievers, and we actively contribute to the knowledge of our field in order to help one another become better scholars, teachers, administrators, and citizens of the world—as well as of our institutions.

Table 7.2. Three Approaches to Improvement

3 Specific Ways to Improve:		What Graduate Students Can Do	What Graduate Programs and the Field Can Do	What Academic Institutions Can Do
1. Develop More Support Resources	Scholarship	Participate in research studies on graduate students and write narratives of your experiences.	Encourage studies on graduate programs and on new faculty. Help create guides and books about the professoriate related specifically to the field.	Ask about and encourage studies on their new faculty, tracking new-faculty needs, and making study findings and needs publicly visible.
	Financial	Learn how to seek and apply for funding, such as grants, stipends, and other kinds.	Encourage faculty to help students with funding opportunities, including conference and activity funding.	Ask about and help develop internal grant funding opportunities, budget proposals, and paid course releases.
	Material	Learn to use the professional position statements put forth by various organizations in our field. Work on professional documents for the job market, even if you won't apply for some time. Update often.	Help develop materials for teaching, researching, serving, and administrating.	Make sure guides and handbooks are provided with clear job descriptions and expectations for new faculty. Develop materials for teaching, researching, serving, and administering in terms of job contracts.
	Time	Learn time-management skills and recognize the scope of activities required of new faculty.	Encourage programs to use position statements from the field that support time management.	Develop requests for paid course releases. Work to establish a balance of responsibilities and have this in writing.

continued on next page

Table 7.2—continued

3 Specific Ways to Improve:		What Graduate Students Can Do	What Graduate Programs and the Field Can Do	What Academic Institutions Can Do
2. Formalize Professional Development	Centers or Department Representative	Help shape the professional-development centers on campuses or the initiatives set forth by department representatives. Take on leadership roles.	Promote position statements from the field that support the kinds of professional development critical to our field. Ask to sit in on and participate in committee work.	Encourage the funding and staffing of centers or department development initiatives, training faculty, and the allowing of faculty time to utilize centers and program initiatives.
	Mentoring Programs	Participate in and help shape mentoring programs.	Participate in mentoring programs through conferences, events, and organizations that are teaching mentoring.	Facilitate mentoring programs that teach all faculty to mentor.
3. Capture the Day-to-Day Life Activities of New Faculty	Experiential Learning	Shadow mentors and other faculty in and out of their programs.	Insist programs and the field do more to make the profession a subject. Promote external practicum experiences with peer institutions like two-year colleges.	Invite new faculty to shadow senior faculty.
		Take on leadership roles, committee work, and other service opportunities.	Develop faculty mentoring beyond program advising. Allow students to choose faculty mentors and provide structure to allow for holistic guidance of the student's journey.	Help align job expectations and descriptions with daily life of faculty.

In the comics *Piled High and Deeper,* Jorge Cham uses common academic experiences to elicit humorous responses from readers. Recurring characters include exploited TAs, dismissive senior colleagues, borderline abusive dissertation advisors, and even a hopeless humanities graduate student who is always trying to convince the institution of the value of his field. It's funny because, sadly, it's true. Jokes about the insanity of pursuing a graduate degree aren't hard to find, and academic culture does little to promote wellness among its faculty and staff, let alone its graduate students. We implore you to consider another way.

What if . . .

HERE ARE QUESTIONS TO CONSIDER . . . *REGARDING YOUR CURRENT SITUATION (AND PROSPECTIVE CAREER)*

Now that you have reached the end of the book, we want to leave you with some questions you can use to reflect on what you can do to improve your situation and the situations of others in our field.

- How can you help your graduate program make changes to better serve current and future students?
- How can you request that the field help provide professional development for graduate students and new faculty?
- How can you impact your future hiring institutions to make faculty's transitions from graduate school to the professoriate successful?

Chimamanda Adichie's TED Talk "The Danger of a Single Story," exposes what misunderstandings proliferate when our understanding of a people or place is based on a single story, a single experience. To some extent, our research points to the fact that a 2/2 position at a research-focused institution could be the "single story" of our professoriate. This book provides a number of activities that encourage you to explore beyond this single story. Now that you have had the opportunity to do so, reflect on the overlapping stories that actually make up the narratives of our profession. Consider what you have learned not only in terms of the discipline but also in terms of your career aspirations as a future professional.

HERE ARE MOVES YOU CAN MAKE TO . . . *HELP GRADUATE PROGRAMS, INSTITUTIONS, AND OUR FIELD*

To summarize the suggestions in this chapter and to help you answer the questions above, the previous table distinguishes some important ways you can help yourself, graduate programs, our field, and hiring institutions specifically.

APPENDIX

Framework

Chapter Framework	Introduction	STRATEGY 1 Know (Y)Our Stories	STRATEGY 2 Understand the Job Market	STRATEGY 3 Define Your Tetrad: TRSA
Here's a Story about . . .	Why We Need More Robust Preparation for the Professoriate	How Our Research Revealed Many Stories	Those on the Job Market	What a New Faculty Member Had to Say about the Tetrad
Here's Our Advice about . . .	Why Doctoral Programs Matter to the Preparation of New Faculty	Understanding How Stories Operate in Our Field	The Job Market Experience	Defining TRSA While Trying to Work at an Institution That is Trying to Define it for You
Here's What Our Research Says about . . .	Choosing the Professoriate as a Career Path	Studying New Faculty	How Participants Felt about the Job Market	The Current State of TRSA for New Faculty
Here's What Scholarship Says about . . .	Similar Studies	Narratives and Storytelling	Jobs	Administrative Work
Here's How We . . .	Organized and Structured this Book	Use Story to Reflect on Professional Identity	Attempt to Obtain a Job	Can Better Serve our Graduate Students
Here Are Questions to Consider . . .	When Reading This Book	When Thinking about Stories	When Putting Together Materials and Choosing the Right Job Position	About the Material Realities of the Tetrad
Here Are Moves You Can Make to . . .	Keep an Open, Positive Mind	Reflect on Your and Others' Stories	Network before You Are on the Job Market	Become More Proficient in All Areas of the Tetrad

https://doi.org/10.7330/9781646421640.c008

STRATEGY 4 Prepare for More than TRSA	*STRATEGY 5* Recognize Your Time Is Valuable and Manage It Well	*STRATEGY 6* Collaborate	*Moving Forward:* Faculty and Graduate Program Support
Making Our Work Visible	Accounting for a Faculty Member's Time	Why Learning to Collaborate in Graduate School Matters	The Future
Trying to Make Visible All You Do	Making Time Work for You	Learning to Collaborate as a Graduate Student	Teaching a Discipline versus Developing a Professional
The Other Things New Faculty Do on the Job	How New Faculty Sometimes Struggle to Balance Workload	What Kinds of Collaboration New Faculty Participate In	The Danger of a Single Story
Research I Institutions and Our Field	Workload	Defining Collaboration	Experiential Learning
Develop a Deeper Understanding of the Job	Can Help Graduate Students Approach Daily Routines More Effectively	Can Foster Collaborative Experiences	Change in Three Specific Ways
When Thinking More Deeply about the TRSA	When Thinking about Time Management	When Entering into Collaborative Experiences	Regarding Your Current Situation (and Prospective Career)
Better Prepare for the Work You Will Do	Develop Time-Management Skills in Graduate School	Collaborate to Make a Difference	Help Graduate Programs, Institutions, and Our Field

WORKS CITED

Addison, Joanne. "Narrative as Method and Methodology in Socially Progressive Research." *Practicing Research in Writing Studies: Reflexive and Ethically Responsible Research*, edited by Katrina M. Powell and Pamela Takayoshi, Hampton, 2012, pp. 373–383.

Adichie, Chimamanda. "The Danger of a Single Story," *TED*, July 2009. https://www.ted.com/talks/chimamanda_ngozi_adichie_the_danger_of_a_single_story?language=en. Accessed 7 Aug. 2021.

Alexander, Jonathan, Susan C. Jarrett, and Nancy Welch, editors. *Unruly Rhetorics: Protest, Persuasion, and Publics*. U of Pittsburgh P, 2018.

Arola, Kristin L., Jennifer Sheppard, and Cheryl E. Ball. *Writer/Designer: A Guide to Making Multimodal Projects*. Bedford/St. Martin's, 2014.

Artze-Vega, Isis, et al. "Privileging Pedagogy: Composition, Rhetoric, and Faculty Development." *College Composition and Communication*, vol. 65, no. 1, 2013, pp. 162–184.

Battershill, Claire, et al. *Scholarly Adventures in Digital Humanities: Making the Modernist Archives Publishing Project*. Palgrave Macmillan, 2017.

Beigi, Mina. "Work-Family Interaction among Faculty: A Systematic Literature Review and a Phenomenological Study." 2015. Texas A&M U, PhD Dissertation.

Bodovski, Katerina. "Why I Collapsed on the Job." *The Chronicle of Higher Education*, 15 Feb. 2018, https://www.chronicle.com/article/Why-I-Collapsed-on-the-Job/242537. Accessed 22 May 2020.

Brems, Brian. "Views on the First Year on the Faculty: Same Ship, Different Perspective." *New to the Faculty: Everything New Professors Need to Know to Be Successful*. The Chronicle of Higher Education, 2018, pp. 26–28.

Bruner, Jerome. *Making Stories: Law, Literature, and Life*. Harvard UP, 2002.

Butler, Judith. *The Psychic Life of Power: Theories in Subjection*. Stanford UP, 1997.

Calhoon-Dillahunt, Carolyn, et al. "TYCA Guidelines for Preparing Teachers of English in the Two-Year College." *Teaching English in the Two-Year College*, vol. 45, no. 1, 2017, pp. 8–19.

Carlo, Rosanne, and Theresa Jarnagin Enos. "Back-Tracking and Forward-Gazing: Making the Dimensions of Graduate Core Curricula in Rhetoric and Composition." *Rhetoric Review*, vol. 30, no. 2, 2011, pp. 208–227. The Chronicle of Higher Education. (Reprinted in *New to the Faculty: Everything New Professors Need to Know to Be Successful*. The Chronicle of Higher Education, 2018.)

Cham, Jorge. *Piled High and Deeper. PhD Comics*, http://phdcomics.com/.

Clandinin, Jean, et al. "Places of Practices: Learning to Think Narratively." *Narrative Works: Issues, Investigations, & Interventions*, vol. 5, no. 1, 2015, pp. 22–39.

https://doi.org/10.7330/9781646421640.c009

"Collaborative Learning and Writing." *Rebecca Moore Howard.* https://www.rebec camoorehoward.com/bibliographies/collaborative-learning-and-writing. Accessed 2 June 2016.

Committee on the Status of Graduate Students. *Report and Recommendations on the Status of Graduate Students.* Conference on College Composition and Communication, 2014, https://prod-ncte-cdn.azureedge.net/nctefiles/groups /cccc/committees/2014sogssurveyreport.pdf.

Conference on College Composition and Communication. "Scholarship in Rhetoric, Writing, and Composition: Guidelines for Faculty, Deans, and Chairs." Conference on College Composition and Communication, Mar. 2018, https://cccc.ncte.org/cccc/resources/positions/scholarshipincomp. Accessed 22 May 2020.

Conference on College Composition and Communication. "CCCC Statement on Preparing Teachers of College Writing." Conference on College Composition and Communication, Nov. 2015, https://cccc.ncte.org/cccc/resources/pos itions/statementonprep. Accessed 22 May 2020.

Conference on College Composition and Communication. "Statement of Professional Guidance for New Faculty Members." Conference on College Composition and Communication, Nov. 2015, https://cccc.ncte.org/cccc /resources/positions/professionalguidance. Accessed 22 May 2020.

Council of Writing Program Administrators. "Evaluating the Intellectual Work of Writing Administration." 17 July 2019, http://wpacouncil.org/aws/CW PA/pt/sd/news_article/242849/_PARENT/layout_details/false. Accessed 22 May 2020.

Coxwell-Teague, Deborah, and Ronald F. Lunsford, editors. *First-Year Composition: From Theory to Practice.* Parlor Press LLC, 2014.

Crisco, Virginia, et al. "Graduate Education as Education: The Pedagogical Arts of Institutional Critique." *Pedagogy,* vol. 3, no. 3, 2003, pp. 359–376.

Dadas, Caroline. "Reaching the Profession: The Locations of the Rhetoric and Composition Job Market" *College Composition and Communication,* vol. 65, no. 1, pp. 67–89.

Dobrin, Sidney I. *Constructing Knowledges: The Politics of Theory-Building and Pedagogy in Composition.* SUNY P, 1997.

Duffy, William. "Collaboration (in) Theory: Reworking the Social Turn's Conversational Imperative." *College English,* vol. 76, no. 5, 2014, pp. 416–435.

Ede, Lisa. *Situating Composition: Composition Studies and the Politics of Location.* Southern Illinois UP, 2004.

Edgington, Anthony, and Stacy Hartlage Taylor. "Invisible Administrators: The Possibilities and Perils of Graduate Student Administration." *WPA: Writing Program Administration,* vol. 31, no. 1–2, 2007, pp. 150–170.

Elder, Cristyn L., et al. "Strengthening Graduate Student Preparation for WPA Work." *WPA: Writing Program Administration,* vol. 37, no. 2, 2014, pp. 13–35.

Farmer, Frank. *After the Public Turn: Composition, Counterpublics, and the Citizen Bricoleur.* Utah State UP, 2013.

Flaherty, Colleen. "The Evolving English Major." *Inside Higher Ed,* 18 Jul 2018, https://www.insidehighered.com/news/2018/07/18/new-analysis-english -departments-says-numbers-majors-are-way-down-2012-its-not-death. Accessed 20 Sep. 2019.

Foley-Schramm, Ashton, et al. "Preparing Graduate Students for the Field: A Graduate Student Praxis Heuristic for WPA Professionalization and Institutional Politics." *WPA: Writing Program Administration*, vol. 40, no. 2, 2018, pp. 89–103.

Gallego, Muriel. "Professional Development of Graduate Teaching Assistants in Faculty-Like Positions: Fostering Reflective Practices through Reflective Teaching Journals." *Journal of the Scholarship of Teaching and Learning*, vol. 14, no. 2, 2014, pp. 96–110.

George, Diana, editor. *Kitchen Cooks, Plate Twirlers, and Troubadours: Writing Program Administrators Tell Their Stories*. Boyton/Cook, 1999.

Giberson, Greg, et al. "A Changing Profession Changing a Discipline: Junior Faculty and the Undergraduate Major." *Composition Forum*, vol. 20, 2009, https://files.eric.ed.gov/fulltext/EJ1080990.pdf. Accessed 7 Aug. 2021.

Glenn, Cheryl, and Melissa A. Goldthwaite. *The St. Martin's Guide to Teaching Writing*. 7th ed. MacMillan, 2014.

Goggin, Maureen Daly, and Peter Goggin. *Serendipity in Rhetoric, Writing, and Literacy Research*, UP of Colorado, 2018.

Gous, Ignatius G. P, and Jennifer J. Roberts. "About Time: A Metacognitive View of Time and Workload Created by Technological Advancements in an ODL Environment." *Distance Education*, vol. 36, no. 2, 2015, pp. 263–281.

Gries, Laurie E. "Writing to Assemble Publics: Making Writing Active, Making Writing Matter." *College Composition and Communication*, vol. 70, no. 3, 2019, pp. 327–355.

Gries, Laurie E, and Collin Gifford Brooke, editors. *Circulation, Writing, and Rhetoric*. Utah State UP, 2018.

Gutierrez de Blume, Antonio P., and Lori L. Candela. "Perceptions of Teaching, Research, and Service Expertise, Workload, Organizational Support, and Satisfaction Among U.S. Faculty Members' Intent to Stay in Tier 1 or Tier 2 Organizations: A Structural Equation Model." *International Journal of Learning, Teaching, and Educational Research*, vol. 17, no. 4, 2018, pp. 1–17.

Hallier, Jerry, and Juliette Summers. "Dilemmas and Outcomes of Professional Identity Construction among Students of Human Resource Management." *Human Resource Management Journal*, vol. 21, no. 2, 2011, pp. 204–219.

Hixson-Bowles, Kelsey, and Enrique Paz. "Perspectives on Collaborative Scholarship." *The Peer Review*, vol. 0, no. 0, 2015, http://thepeerreview-iwca.org/issues/issue-0/perspectives-on-collaborative-scholarship/. Accessed 4 Oct. 2019.

Hjortshoj, Keith. *From Student to Scholar: A Guide to Writing Through the Dissertation Stage*. Routledge, 2019.

Holt, Mara. *Collaborative Learning as Democratic Practice: A History*. NCTE, 2018. CCCC Studies in Rhetoric and Writing.

Howard, Rebecca Moore. "Why This Humanist Codes." *Research in the Teaching of English*, vol. 49, no. 1, 2014, pp. 75–81.

Hult, Christine, and the Portland Resolution Committee. "Evaluating the Intellectual Work of Writing Program Administration." *WPA: Writing Program Administration*, vol. 16, no. 1–2, 1992, pp. 88–94.

Jacobs, Gloria E. "Troubling Research: A Field Journey through Methodological Decision Making." *Practicing Research in Writing Studies: Reflexive and Ethically*

Responsible Research, edited by Katrina M. Powell and Pamela Takayoshi, Hampton, 2012, pp. 331–347.

Jacobs, Jerry A., and Sarah E. Winslow. "Overworked Faculty: Job Stresses and Family Demands." *The Annals of the American Academy of Political and Social Science*, vol. 596, no. 1, 2004, pp. 104–129.

Jiménez, Javier. "My First Semester on the Tenure Track." *New to the Faculty: Everything New Professors Need to Know to Be Successful*. The Chronicle of Higher Education, 2018, pp. 13–14. Originally published in *The Chronicle of Higher Education*, 10 January 2013. https://www.chronicle.com/article/my-first-semester-on-the-tenure-track/. Accessed 7 Aug. 2021.

Journet, Debra. "Narrative Turns in Writing Studies Research." *Writing Studies Research in Practice: Methods and Methodologies*, edited by Lee Nickoson and Mary P. Sheridan, Southern Illinois UP, 2012, pp. 13–24.

Keller, Elizabeth J. "About Me." 2019, http://beth-keller.com/. Accessed 27 Feb. 2019.

Keller, Elizabeth J. *Rhetorical Strategies for Professional Development: Investment Mentoring in Classrooms and Workplaces*. Routledge, 2018.

Kezar, Adrianna, et al. "The Professoriate Reconsidered: A Study of New Faculty Models." Oct. 2015, https://pullias.usc.edu/wp-content/uploads/2015/10/Professoriate-Reconsidered-final.pdf. Accessed 22 May 2020.

Kilfoil, Carrie Byers. "Beyond the 'Foreign' Language Requirement: From a Monolingual to a Translingual Ideology in Rhetoric and Composition Graduate Education." *Rhetoric Review*, vol. 34, no. 4, 2015, pp. 426–444.

Kolb, Alice Y., and David A. Kolb. "Learning Styles and Learning Spaces: Enhancing Experiential Learning in Higher Education." *Academy of Management Learning & Education*, vol. 4, no. 2, June 2005, pp. 193–212.

Kramnick, Jonathan. "What We Hire in Now: English by the Grim Numbers." *The Chronicle of Higher Education*, 9 Dec 2018, https://www.chronicle.com/article/What-We-Hire-in-Now-English/245255. Accessed 20 Sep. 2019.

Laurence, David. "The Latest Forecast." *ADE Bulletin*, no. 131, Spring 2002, pp. 14–19.

Link, Albert N., et al. "A Time Allocation Study of University Faculty." *Economics of Education Review*, vol. 27, no. 4, 2008, pp. 363–374.

Lunsford, Andrea A., and Lisa Ede. *Writing Together: Collaboration in Theory and Practice*. Bedford/St. Martin's, 2012.

Mann, Steve. *The Research Interview: Reflective Practice and Reflexivity in Research Processes*. Palgrave, 2016.

Mathieu, Paula. "Excavating Indoor Voices: Inner Rhetoric and the Mindful Writing Teacher." *JAC*, vol. 34, no. 1–2, 2014, pp. 173–190.

Mendenhall, Annie S. "The Composition Specialist as Flexible Expert: Identity and Labor in the History of Composition." *College English*, vol. 77, no. 1, 2014, pp. 11–31.

Miller, Scott L., et al. "Present Perfect and Future Imperfect: Results of a National Survey of Graduate Students in Rhetoric and Composition Programs." *College Composition and Communication*, vol. 48, no. 3, 1997, pp. 392–409.

"MLA Survey of Departmental Staffing, Fall 2014," Modern Language Association, 2014, https://www.mla.org/content/download/103529/2303971/2014-Staffing-Survey.pdf. Accessed 22 May 2020.

Mutnick, Deborah. "Inscribing the World: Lessons from an Oral History Project in Brooklyn." *College Composition and Communication*, vol. 66, no. 4, 2015, pp. 626–647.

National Center for Faculty Development & Diversity. "How to Thrive in Academia." 2019, https://facultydiversity.org. Accessed 19 June 2019.

National Society for Experiential Education. "Eight Principles of Good Practice for All Experiential Learning Activities." 2013. https://www.nsee.org/8 -principles. Accessed 7 May 2019.

Perlmutter, David D. "Good Deeds That Are Most Punished: Teaching." *New to the Faculty: Everything New Professors Need to Know to Be Successful*. The Chronicle of Higher Education, 2018, pp. 17–19. Originally published in *The Chronicle of Higher Education*, 6 Feb. 2012. https://www.chronicle.com/ article/Good-Deeds-That-Are-Most/130649. Accessed 10 Oct. 2019.

Perlmutter, David D. "Good Deeds That Are Most Punished: Service." *New to the Faculty: Everything New Professors Need to Know to Be Successful.* The Chronicle of Higher Education, 2018, pp. 20–22. Originally published in *The Chronicle of Higher Education*, 25 Mar. 2012. https://www.chronicle.com/article/good -deeds-that-are-most-punished-service/. Accessed 10 Oct. 2019.

Pratt, Michael G., et al. "Constructing Professional Identity: The Role of Work and Identity Learning Cycles in the Customization of Identity among Medical Residents." *Academy of Management Journal*, vol. 49, no. 2, 2006, pp. 235–262.

Reid, E. Shelley. "Mentoring Peer Mentors: Mentor Education and Support in the Composition Program." *Composition Studies*, vol. 36, no. 2, 2008, pp. 51–79.

"Report on the MLA *Job Information List*, 2016–2017." Modern Language Association, 2017, https://www.mla.org/content/download/78816/2172744/Re port-MLA-JIL-2016-17.pdf. Accessed 15 April 2018.

Reybold, Earle L., and Jennifer J. Alamia. "Academic Transitions in Education: A Developmental Perspective of Women Faculty Experiences." *Journal of Career Development*, vol. 35, no. 2, 2008, pp. 107–128.

Rivers, Nathaniel. "Geocomposition in Public Rhetoric and Writing Pedagogy." *College Composition and Communication*, vol. 67, no. 4, 2016, pp. 576–606.

Sano-Franchini, Jennifer. "'It's Like Writing Yourself into a Codependent Relationship with Someone Who Doesn't Even Want You!': Emotional Labor, Intimacy, and the Academic Job Market in Rhetoric and Composition" *College Composition and Communication*, vol. 68, no. 1, 2016. pp. 98–124.

Savage, Karen, and Dominic Symonds. *Economies of Collaboration in Performance: More Than the Sum of the Parts*. Springer, 2018.

Skeffington, Jillian K. "Situating Ourselves: The Development of Doctoral Programs in Rhetoric and Composition." *Rhetoric Review*, vol. 30, no. 1, 2010, pp. 54–71.

Slay, Holly S., and Delmonize A. Smith. "Professional Identity Construction: Using Narrative to Understand the Negotiation of Professional and Stigmatized Cultural Identities." Interdisciplinary Approaches to Contemporary Career Studies, special issue of *Human Relations*, vol. 64, no. 1, 2011, pp. 85–107.

Stein, Mari-Klara, et al. "Towards an Understanding of Identity and Technology in the Workplace." *Journal of Information Technology*, vol. 28, no. 3, 2013, pp. 167–182.

Stenberg, Shari J. *Professing and Pedagogy: Learning the Teaching of English*. NCTE, 2005.

"Strategic Plan." *POD Network*, 2019, https://podnetwork.org/about-us/mission/. Accessed 15 May 2020.

The Successful President of Tomorrow: The 5 Skills Future Leaders Will Need. The Chronicle of Higher Education, May 2019.

Takayoshi, Pamela, et al. "The Construction of Research Problems and Methods." *Practicing Research in Writing Studies: Reflexive and Ethically Responsible Research*, edited by Katrina M. Powell and Pamela Takayoshi, Hampton, 2012, pp. 97–121.

Tulley, Christine E. *How Writing Faculty Write: Strategies for Process, Product, and Productivity*. UP of Colorado, 2018.

Twale, Darla J. *A Faculty Guide for Succeeding in Academe*. Routledge, 2013.

University of Southern California Pullias Center for Higher Education. "The Delphi Project on the Changing Faculty and Student Success: National Trends for Faculty Composition Over Time." PDF, 2012. https://pullias.usc.edu/wp-content/uploads/2012/05/Delphi-NTTF_National-Trends-for-Faculty-Composition_WebPDF.pdf. Accessed 7 Aug. 2021.

US Department of Education, Institute of Education Sciences and the National Center for Education Statistics. *The Condition of Education 2017*. By Joel McFarland, et al. 2017. https://nces.ed.gov/pubs2017/2017144.pdf. Accessed 15 Apr. 2018.

VanHaitsma, Pamela, and Steph Ceraso. "'Making It' in the Academy Through Horizontal Mentoring." *Peitho Journal*, vol 19, no. 2, 2017, pp. 211–233.

Warner, Michael. *Publics and Counterpublics*. Zone, 2005.

Yancey, Kathleen Blake, and Michael Spooner. "A Single Good Mind: Collaboration, Cooperation, and the Writing Self." *College Composition and Communication*, vol. 49, no. 1, 1998, pp. 45–62.

Ziker, John. "The Long, Lonely Job of Homo Academicus." *The Blue Review*, 31 March 2014, https://thebluereview.org/faculty-time-allocation/. Accessed 4 Sep. 2018.

INDEX

ABOUT THE AUTHORS

Claire Lutkewitte, PhD, is a professor of writing in the Department of Communication, Media, and the Arts in the Halmos College of Arts and Sciences at Nova Southeastern University. She teaches a variety of undergraduate and graduate courses including basic writing, college writing, writing with technologies, teaching writing, and research methods. She has published four books, *Writing in a Technological World*, *Mobile Technologies and the Writing Classroom*, *Multimodal Composition: A Critical Sourcebook*, and *Web 2.0: Applications for Composition Classrooms*. Currently, she is working on a book chapter on professionalizing multimodal composition.

Juliette C. Kitchens, PhD, is an associate professor of writing in the Department of Communication, Media, and the Arts in the Halmos College of Arts and Sciences and serves as the Director of Graduate Studies. She teaches a range of composition courses, courses in the writing minor, and graduate courses in the MA in Composition, Rhetoric, and Digital Media. Her research interests include identity studies, rhetorics of popular culture, rhetorics of technologies, and postprocess pedagogies. She has published two books, *At Home in the Whedonverse: Essays on Domestic Place, Space, and Life* and *Transmediating the Whedonverse(s): Essays on Texts, Paratexts, and Metatexts*.

Molly J. Scanlon, PhD, is an associate professor in the Department of Communication, Media, and the Arts in the Halmos College of Arts and Sciences at Nova Southeastern University. She teaches a variety of undergraduate courses in composition and university (UNIV) first-year seminars. She also teaches research methods and visual media to graduate students in the MA in Composition, Rhetoric, and Digital Media. Dr. Scanlon's research interests center on visual rhetoric and rhetorics of identity. Her work is published in *Composition Studies*, *Reflections*, *ImageText*, and the *Journal of Faculty Development*.